D0249778

Bound for JOY

Philippians— Paul's Letter from Prison

STUART BRISCOE

Regal Books
A Division of GL Publications
Ventura, California, U.S.A.

Other good reading in this series:

When the Going Gets Tough (1 Peter)
    by Stuart Briscoe
Themes from Isaiah
    by Ronald Youngblood
From Trials to Triumphs (James)
    by Derek Prime
Love Carved in Stone (10 Commandments)
    by Daniel R. Seagren

The translation of all Regal books is under the direction of GLINT. GLINT provides technical help for the adaptation, translation and publishing of books for millions of people worldwide. For information regarding translation contact: GLINT, P.O. Box 6688, Ventura, California 93006.

Scripture quotations are from the *Authorized King James Version.*

Revised edition

Published by Regal Books
A Division of GL Publications
Ventura, California 93006
Printed in U.S.A.

Library of Congress Cataloging in Publication Data

Briscoe, D. Stuart.
    Bound for joy.

    (A Bible commentary for laymen)
    1. Bible. N.T. Philippians—Commentaries.
    I. Title. II. Series.
BS2705.3.B74   1984   227'.6077   84-17778
ISBN 0-8307-1004-3

CONTENTS

A Gospel Light Teacher's Manual and Student Discovery Guide for Bible study groups using *Bound for Joy* are available from your church supplier.

1
I'M SO HAPPY HERE IN PRISON

Paul and Timotheus, the servants of Jesus Christ, to all the saints in Christ Jesus which are at Philippi, with the bishops and deacons: Grace be unto you, and peace, from God our Father and from the Lord Jesus Christ. I thank my God upon every remembrance of you, always in every prayer of mine for you all making request with joy, for your fellowship in the gospel from the first day until now; being confident of this very thing, that he which hath begun a good work in you will perform it until the day of Jesus Christ. Even as it is meet for me to think this of you all, because I have you in my heart; inasmuch as both in my bonds, and in the defense and confirmation of the gospel, ye all are partakers of my grace. For God is my record, how greatly I long after you all in the bowels of Jesus Christ. And this I pray, that your love may abound yet more and more in knowledge and in all judgment; that ye may approve things that are excellent; that ye may be sincere and without offense till the day of Christ; being filled with the fruits of righteousness, which are by Jesus Christ, unto the glory and praise of God.

Philippians 1:1-11

Paul wrote the Philippian letter a from prison, possibly in Rome or Ephesus or Caesarea. It is easy to overlook this fact because the tone of Paul's letter is so positive, and the subject matter so outgoing.

Paul talks a lot about "joy" and "rejoicing." Not the "I've got a wonderful feeling, everything's going my way" kind of joy, but a remarkable joy that he could experience in prison when things were going wrong. That is a quality of life that is worth knowing, because we all have our prisons of one kind or another.

Happy Memories

Happy memories were partially responsible for Paul's ability to rejoice in jail. He did not sit in his place of confinement feeling sorry for himself. Rather, he said, "I thank my God upon every remembrance of you ... . with joy" (vv. 3,4). "Every remembrance" means literally "my total recollection of you."

Paul's memories of the days in Philippi brought him joy. He remembered fondly the girl who had the demon problem. He remembered with joy the jailer who beat him up. He thought of being chained to the slimy wall of the cell as the earth beneath him quaked. And as he remembered the experience, he had a great sense of joy. Lydia, the skilled businesswoman, and her group of faithful women came to his mind, and he remembered with great joy his association with them.

As he thought of them all, one thing captivated his mind. God had been at work in those days in Philippi; He had worked during the pleasant times by the river and the ugly times in the cell, the placid days of prayer and teaching, and the fearful days of pain and terror. In fact, God had done such a beautiful work in the lives of the Philippian believers that they had joined Paul in his evangelism "from the first day," and they had kept it up "until now."

God had so changed their attitudes that instead of

being in opposition to Paul, they had built up a close and loving relationship with him. "I have you in my heart" (v. 7) could also be translated, "You have me in your heart." There was a two-way relationship of love. In fact, Paul went so far as to say, "I long after you all in the bowels (affections) of Jesus Christ" (v. 8). This strange-sounding statement means, "I have a heartache for you." It's an idea that used to be expressed in the phrase "a passion for souls." It means a "burden"—a heart that aches for those in need. "Bowels" really means "heart." Paul is saying he loves these people with the love of Christ.

When you find yourself in prison, or in a hospital bed, or tied to a kitchen sink, or anchored to an office desk, it's a good thing to remember what God has been doing in your life instead of moaning about your present status. That will remind you of what He is committed to doing, and your prison, like Charles Wesley's, may "flame with light."

Happy Prayers

Happy prayers were also part of Paul's life in prison. His prayers were not impassioned pleadings to be released or whining inquiries as to why God had made the mistake of allowing these things to happen. His prayers were not self-centered prayers at all. "Always in every prayer of mine *for you* all making request . . . " (v. 4). Neither were they formal intonings, but rather prayers prayed "with joy."

Love's Description

Paul was particularly concerned about the love aspect of the Philippians' Christian experience. So he said, "This I pray, that your love might abound yet more and more" (v. 9).

The word *agape* is the Greek word Paul chose to use for love. Not *phileo* from which we get "Philadelphia" and "philanthropic"; not *eros* from which we get our over-worked word "erotic." No, Paul chose *agape*, the word used to describe God's love. It takes the knowledge of God and the power of God's Spirit to produce *agape*. Man can love with *phileo* on his own, and *eros* is pretty easy to come by. But the "love of God" is something quite distinctive, and it is this *agape* love that Paul was anxious to see in the lives of the Philippian believers.

The best way to understand what Paul was hoping to see in them is to read the best known verse of the Bible. "God so loved . . . that he gave . . . " (John 3:16). The essence of *agape* is giving. God's *agape* drove Him to give and give and go on giving.

I am convinced that our understanding of love is inadequate today. For many, it is soft lights, sweet music, sentimentality and romanticism. The giving of Christ was not done to soft lights and sweet music. It was enacted on a cross to the accompaniment of jeers and curses, and it had its crashing crescendo in the words, "Father forgive them . . . " That is *agape*.

There is one thing that could revolutionize modern society faster than anything else: *agape*. If hatred was attacked by love, and antagonism was countered with love, and people started giving instead of grabbing, reaching outward rather than growing inward, building bridges instead of barriers, our world would wonder what had happened. Society would be shocked.

Paul's prayer is simply that the Christians in Philippi might initiate this kind of shock. The same thing applies today, and the same revolutionary love is desperately needed in our secular world, and it has to start in the church of Jesus Christ.

Love's Distribution
Note carefully the words, "abound yet more and more." Paul really prayed intensely at this point. He could

have stopped at "abound," or at "more," but he wanted to make his point clear. He wanted their love to "abound yet more and more." He was anxious that their love should have no bounds, that it would overflow in a great demonstration of God's activity in their lives.

Someone told me one day, "I have a lot of love to give, but I don't know to whom I should give it." Abounding *agape* doesn't worry about such problems. It is rather like a bottle of well-shaken pop. It bursts out in a every direction! Let's think of some of these directions.

First, *agape* abounds *deeper.* When a young couple get married they usually sit at the reception after the ceremony oblivious to their guests. They are starry-eyed and wrapped up in each other. Try telling them that their love is shallow, and they'll probably hit you with the wedding cake! But ask them ten years later if their love has grown deeper. If all has gone well they will answer in the affirmative and say, "We are just discovering something of the depth of love." That's how it is with *agape*. As love deepens, it grows up.

Take the story of the Prodigal Son for instance. The young son usually gets the glory, but the old father is the hero in my opinion. He demonstrated deep love in the greatness of his forgiveness. The longer he had to wait for his son's return, the more he loved him. As he suffered more, his capacity for love deepened. His love didn't waver or die. It kept on flowing. The deeper it flowed, the more it endured.

Second, love can abound *wider. Agape* is not exclusive. "God so loved the world . . . " There's nothing exclusive about a world-embracing love. Our love can become restricted to those we like, to those who like us, to those we would very much like to have like us!

We can love the lovely, the lovable and the loving. But that isn't *agape*. God's love flowed to a world of God haters, and embraced every one of them. Paul's prayer that the Philippians' love might abound undoubtedly included the idea of their love becoming less exclusive. He wanted their love to be so wide that it would not insist on the right to be selective or require assurance that it would be reciprocated. *Agape* love is wide enough to love the unloved and the unlovely.

A critic of Christianity told me that he thought the church was full of kooks, and he didn't want his children associating with kooks. I couldn't agree that the church is full of odd people, but I gladly agreed that one usually finds a higher percentage of odd people in the church than in any other place where people meet voluntarily. And, quite frankly, I was glad that he had noticed this. I thanked him for what he had intended as a slur and pointed out that in actual fact it was a beautiful compliment. What a joy to be a member of a society that has more than her fair share of the unfortunate! *Agape* love is wide enough to welcome this unfortunate in large numbers.

Corrie ten Boom, the Dutch woman who suffered terribly in the concentration camps of the Second World War, exemplified a love that grows wider and wider. Her love grew so wide that she learned to forgive and to love some of those responsible for the misery she endured in the camps. *Agape* love is wide enough to love the hateful, too.

Few of us, if any, will be thrown into a concentration camp to see if we can demonstrate abounding love. Don't let that worry you, because you will find plenty of opportunities outside concentration camps! You can show love to the secretary who fouled up your airline reservations, or the boss who cancelled your vacation, or the husband who said no to your suggestion about eating out!

Third, love can abound in a *fuller* sense. Deeper love will endure more, wider love will embrace more, but fuller love will risk more.

There is always an element of risk in love. Love may be given but not returned. That is a terribly humbling

experience, but the risk must be taken. Love may motivate to action, but others may attribute ulterior motives to
the action. This is an infuriating experience, but, here
again, the risk must be taken. Spurned and misunderstood
love is the hardest kind of love to maintain. That is why so
often love dies when it is not appreciated. Rather than
fight the battle of rejection and risk the embarrassment of
misunderstanding, it just quits. But not *agape,* in its fulness. *Agape* goes on and insists on abounding.

It isn't surprising that Paul could be happy in prison
when we realize that his heart was in tune with heaven
through prayer, and the subject of his prayer was that
most delightful of subjects, love.

Love's Discipline

Love and discipline sound strange when coupled
together. Love sounds like violins and roses, while discipline conjures up pictures of drums and bayonets. But
they do belong together, and to forget this is disastrous.
Note that Paul prayed: " . . . that your love may abound
. . . in knowledge and . . . judgment" (v. 9).

To love with knowledge means that you don't allow
your heart to rule your head. And to love with judgment
means that your love does not deaden your critical facul-
ties. Love may be blind, but *agape* has 20/20 vision.

Have you ever met a child who was the product of a
misguided parental upbringing? I'm thinking of the kind of
child whose parents spoiled him because they thought that
their love for him would be questioned if they ever denied
him anything. As a result, he got everything he wanted
whether he needed it or not, and grew up to be a young
person with no sense of values. He never learned the difference between wants and needs. Eventually he became
so confused that he mistook wants for needs and needs for
rights, till in the end he was insufferable. Parental love
must be according to "knowledge and judgment."

The love that invariably says yes is not necessarily *agape* showing discretion. It may be immature love copping out of an argument or selfish love refusing to confront possible unpopularity.

Many a pastor has shown his "love" for his people by saying nothing about their sin. In this he was wrong. His noble calling is to love them but to denounce their sin. Love disciplines with adequate understanding and realistic evaluation. If it does not, then the quality of love is suspect.

In the '60s, young people of the counterculture had a great impact on modern society. Much of their impact has been for good. They dared to talk about love, and they did something about it. They wrote "love" on the front of their sweat shirts and "peace" on the back. Noble sentiments and glorious aspirations, but their Utopian dreams crumbled around their ears because they didn't understand that Utopia becomes hell if discipline is not experienced.

Some ecumenists have insisted on loving everybody regardless of their theological position, and this is admirable. But their love has not only embraced people who deny some of the fundamentals of the faith, but has also embraced their error. They lacked the discipline that would say in love, "So far and no further." As a result, their love in its misguided form has not produced a virile witness to Christ, but rather an enemic blend of truth and error.

There should be no conflict in the Christian's mind concerning the necessity of love's discipline. "Whom the Lord loveth he chasteneth" (Heb. 12:6), seems to be perfectly clear to those who are open to hear what it is saying.

Some years ago I spoke to a large group of high school students at a summer camp. Some of them behaved badly all week, but as I was the junior member of the team of speakers, I waited for some of my elders to deal with the situation. On the final day of the conference it became apparent that they were not going to say anything. So I did!

I told the group that most of them had been courteous and attentive, but a few of them had not. I said that the next ten minutes would apply only to those who didn't know how to behave in a worship service, and I knew six of the large crowd who fitted into that category. So that there wouldn't be any doubt about who they were, I pointed them out. Then I proceeded.

At the end of my talk a young giant came bustling up to me with a red face and shouted, "Were you talking to me?"

"You know perfectly well that I was talking to you," I replied.

There was a pause and then his face crumpled and he said, "Gee, thanks. You're the first person who cared enough about me to tell me where I was wrong."

About four years later, as I was registering new students in an English Bible school, a young lady said to me, "Do you remember me?"

"Sorry," I replied, "I'm afraid I don't."

"You should," she went on, "because you pointed me out in a crowd of kids in a youth conference four years ago. I did not appreciate it at the time, but I decided then that if ever I wanted to go for training in the Christian life I would go to a place where they care enough about young people to discipline them."

Love exercises discipline and discernment in its associations and relationships. Paul expressed it beautifully: "that ye may approve things that are excellent" (v. 10). Probably it would be easier for us to understand this phrase if we translate it, "test things that differ." Your love should be able to differentiate between a genuine need that you should attempt to meet, and a phony pitch that you should attempt to expose. Love should recognize the difference between emotional stress to be reached out to, and selfish egotism to be rebuked.

Love should also know how to consistently love sinners and consistently hate sin. It's too easy for Christians to get it all the wrong way around, to hate sinners and to love their sin. But our Lord gave us a perfect example of how it was to be done. He knew the difference between Mary Magdalene's sin and her crushing need. He saw behind the grasping greed of Zacchaeus and knew the empty heart that longed for love.

Love's Distinctive

Paul's prayer went on, "that ye may be sincere and without offense . . . " (v. 10). The Greek word translated "sincere" is a word that means "unmixed, or without alloy." Some metals in their original state contain many impurities and need to be smelted to purify them. Paul wants the Philippians' love to be so refined in the crucible of spiritual experience that it will be distinctive in its obvious sincerity and reality.

Soon after my wife and I arrived in the United States we received a letter offering us two pairs of nylons. Then two young men arrived at the door and insisted on giving my wife the nylons. She, being British and suspicious, was uneasy, so she asked them, "Why do you want to give me, a complete stranger, something like this?"

"It's our pleasure to give you this gift because you are new to our area," they replied.

"But I don't really want to accept them from you. I don't know you, and I know of no reason why you should give them to me," she insisted.

"Well," said one young man, "surely you will accept a gift from us so that we can demonstrate to you our new vacuum cleaner."

Then it was perfectly clear! They didn't want to give a gift, they wanted to sell a product.

It is this kind of manipulation of people posing as love and concern that has produced a generation of cynics in our day. If someone offers something for nothing, the first thought that comes into our heads is, "What's the catch?" Years ago a man sat on London Bridge offering "a pound for a penny." He got no takers, just suspicious glances from hundreds of passersby.

Sincere, unmixed, unalloyed people are quite distinctive, for they love for Christ's sake and do things for His glory. No catch, and no strings attached. Their love is genuine, and their concern is real. This is *agape* in action.

I'm not surprised, therefore, that Paul was happy in prison. Are you? With all those happy memories reminding him of God's power at work, and all those prayers about love, it would have been surprising if he had been unhappy.

Happy Prospects

He anticipated with great confidence the ongoing work of Christ in the lives of the Philippians. "Being confident of this very thing, that he which hath begun a good work in you will perform it until the day of Jesus Christ" (v. 6). This glorious vote of confidence is worth looking into because it is this kind of confidence that makes happy prisoners.

First, Paul recognized "the work of Christ" in the Philippians' lives. Sometimes I think that we talk a little too glibly about Christ's work in our lives. To really believe that the Lord from heaven is at work in a tiny little life is either arrogant nonsense or magnificent truth. A convinced Christian, of course, rules out the nonsense theory and is locked in to the truth theory. But to take this lightly is to do a massive truth grave injustice.

Whenever the Lord did anything in terms of work, it was superb and it was masterly. And I believe that He has not changed. Therefore, I am dissatisfied with anything that claims to be related to the work of Christ in a person's life that does not bear the stroke of His genius.

His work in regeneration is not a work that produces a shallow decision, but a deep revolution. His activity in conviction produces broken and contrite hearts, not crocodile tears. And that is only the beginning.

Paul's statement here is that if Christ has started something He is not about to quit before He has finished it. He has commenced, and He intends to continue. Herein is a great truth. The beginning of spiritual experience is not the end, nor is the birth from above the complete life. There is work to be done, and the motivating and driving force of this work is the One who started the whole thing in the first place.

It just isn't good enough to be satisfied with a work of Christ that saves from hell but leaves one happy to go on living there. Nor is it satisfactory to be forgiven for failure to produce fruit to the glory of God, and then be perfectly satisfied to go on as fruitless as ever.

When Jesus Christ gets involved in a person's life He wants to finish what He has started. Paul leaves no doubts in the minds of the Philippians that this is what the Lord Jesus had in mind when He entered their lives. And Paul is excited about it.

But he goes on even further, and insists that the Lord has not only commenced in order to continue, but He continues in order to complete. The end product of a redeemed life is another person in the image of God. The finished work of the Lord Jesus is another sinner who has been transformed and is new just like Him. God the Father is committed to this, Jesus Christ His Son is committed to this, and so is the Holy Spirit. Nothing will shake them in their resolve to bring to glorious consummation the work of redemption.

Paul thought long and often and talked much about the "day of Christ" (vv. 6,10). The day of Christ is a term that relates to the Old Testament phrase, "the day of the Lord." It speaks of the inevitable day of divine triumph.

This is the day for which the risen Lord has waited at the Father's right hand, the day for which the saints have labored, the day when the Church will be complete and Christ will come with great glory.

Needless to say, there are many who do not look to the future with glad anticipation. Despair and apprehension characterize the attitudes with which many of our contemporaries contemplate the future. They are afraid and unsure, bewildered and pessimistic. And well they might be, for if Christ is not the risen Lord of glory and His Father the Omnipotent One, then the world is hell-bent for destruction and the universe for disaster.

On the other hand, if Christ is committed to return to take His people home, there is great joy and gladness in the thought and untold confidence in the hearts of all who believe.

There is also a sense of urgency, for no consistent child of God can believe that Christ will come and not tell people to be ready. A Christian who believes, really believes, in the day of Christ has no lack of missionary vision and evangelistic zeal. The doctrine of the day of Christ does that for a person.

The day of Christ has also meant much to Paul because he longed to see his Lord face to face. Having served Him so long and so faithfully he looked for the greeting, "Well done, good and faithful servant," that would make the pain and the hardship of a lifetime of pioneer activity seem like a daydream. He had many a happy hour as he dwelt on the prospects that awaited him.

That is how to be happy in prison. May I suggest that you do what Paul did in his cell. First concentrate on every happy memory that reminds you of the way in which God has worked in your experience. Then engage in prayer that joyfully asks of Him blessings from His bountiful hand. Pray that those you know may deepen and broaden in their love.

Finally, look forward to the great day when Christ shall come. Your prison will not change, but you will. And it may be that, like Paul, you will have a bigger impact on your prison than your prison will have on you.

Questions for Discussion

1. Examine the birth of the Philippian church in Acts 16. What light does this background information shed on the opening chapter of Philippians?

2. Contrast Paul's greeting in Philippians 1:1-2 with similar greetings in the books of Ephesians, Galatians, Colossians, and Romans. How do these passages compare? How are they different?

3. How does Paul's prayer that the Philippians' love would abound relate to his chapter on love in 1 Corinthians 13?

4. Where does love end and confrontation begin? Can the two be reconciled?

5. What effect does God's promise to "complete His work" have upon your life?

THE THINGS THAT HAPPENED TO ME

But I would ye should understand brethren, that the things which happened unto me have fallen out rather unto the furtherance of the gospel; so that my bonds in Christ are manifest in all the palace, and in all other places; and many of the brethren in the Lord, waxing confident by my bonds, are much more bold to speak the word without fear. Some indeed preach Christ even of envy and strife; and some also of good will: The one preach Christ of contention, not sincerely, supposing to add affliction to my bonds; but the other of love, knowing that I am set for the defense of the gospel. What then? notwithstanding, every way, whether in pretense or in truth, Christ is preached; and I therein do rejoice, yea, and will rejoice. For I know that this shall turn to my salvation through your prayer, and the supply of the Spirit of Jesus Christ, according to my earnest expectation and my hope, that in nothing I shall be ashamed, but that with all boldness, as always, so now also Christ shall be magnified in my body, whether it be by life or by death. For to me to live is Christ and to die is gain. But if I live in the flesh, this is the fruit of my labor: yet what I shall choose I wot not. For I am in a strait betwixt two, having a desire to depart, and to be with Christ; which is far better: Nevertheless to abide in the flesh is more needful for you. And having this confidence, I know that I shall abide and continue with you all for your furtherance and joy of faith; that your rejoicing may be more abundant in Jesus Christ for me by my coming to you again.

Philippians 1:12-26

One Sunday morning I was rushing through the church parking lot dispensing cheery greetings to the people as they made their way into the sanctuary. I had no time to hear the answers to such questions as, "How long are you going to be home?" "How did you hurt your leg?" or "How's your mother doing?"

Then one elderly saint with a twinkle in her eye answered my question, "How are you today?" with the words, "How long have you got? You don't have time to hear how I am today, because if I told you all the things that have happened to me recently you wouldn't get into the service."

Mildly rebuked, I thanked her for showing me the emptiness of my question and the lack of interest in my attitude, and I did some serious thinking. The things that happen to me or to you are of great interest to me or to you, but usually they are not as interesting to others. Perhaps this is because when some people talk about the things that happen to them they are simply on another ego trip. But some people have valuable experiences to share, and we should be interested enough to hear them and to learn from their experiences.

The Things That Happened to Me

Paul shows how the things that happened to him had great repercussions in the lives of many people and in the ongoing of the gospel outreach. He firmly believed that things could only happen to him if God permitted them to happen. He was convinced that God would not permit meaningless things to happen to him, and so he looked for the divine purpose in all that took place. He had discovered that things happened *to* him in order that things should happen *in* him. And things happened in him so that things could happen *through* him.

For example, there was the happening of his imprisonment. In verse 13 he talks about "my bonds"—the chains that bound him to his prison wall. Never were chains more restricting than his, or bars more frustrating than those. He had a keenly developed sense of calling and commission. He was the Apostle to the Gentiles, the pioneer missionary, the visionary leader and motivator supreme. But his chains held him. The world was waiting to be conquered by his message, but his message appeared to be conquered by his chains. Yet he regarded his chains as God-sent chains, chains full of purpose. They undoubtedly taught him many things.

The Discipline of Delay

Paul believed that Christ would return in his lifetime. He had a vision of what needed to be done before that event, and he was quite convinced that much of it was not being done. There were so many people to teach and train, to motivate and mobilize, so much to be done and so little being accomplished. It would have been easy for him to become bitter and cynical about the providence of God. But instead, he learned a valuable lesson. He learned that God always works according to His own schedule. Paul calls it "the fulness of the time" (Gal. 4:4).

One of the great Christian disciplines is learning to move at God's speed and in the direction of His movement. The discipline comes to lazy Christians through rebuke and challenge to "awake out of sleep," but to firebrands like Paul it comes through divinely organized delays.

Getting ahead of God through overeagerness can be as disastrous to God's planning as getting behind God through laziness. The discipline of delay is vitally necessary for some.

My wife Jill had an interesting experience of this some years ago. She had planned to use our car one day, but I inadvertently took the car keys with me. Jill was understandably frustrated, as she had particularly asked me to be sure not to do this. However, it was done and could not be undone, so she prayed about her day, including the fact that I had gone off with the car keys and she would not be able to use the car. She committed the day to the Lord and asked Him to work despite the delay.

Two hours later Jill was able to find another car key, so she set off on her journey. Almost immediately she picked up some girl hitchhikers who were bound for London. She discovered that they were German girls and, as she was going to a youth center where many German young people were meeting in a Christian conference, she invited them to go with her. After much debate and numerous refusals they finally agreed to go. As a result, one of these girls committed her life to Christ. Afterwards she told us her story.

She was a theological student in Germany. She had come under the influence of some teaching that, instead of leading her to an intelligent worship of God, had filled her with much doubt and confusion. She had delivered an ultimatum to the God whose existence she doubted. She told God that if He was there He should show Himself to her in some way. He must do this within three months. If He didn't, she told Him, "I'll quit my schooling, quit theology, quit religion, and I *think* I'm going to quit living because there's nothing to live for."

After explaining this, she turned to my wife with great emotion and said, "The three months end today." Delays can teach some mighty lessons when they are accepted as being from God and used for His glory.

The Discipline of Discomfort

Paul had been a brilliant student, taught in the best universities of his day. He far outstripped his academic rivals and had great administrative abilities and remarkable powers of leadership. When he was a fiery opponent of Christ, he motivated thousands to go along with him. And when he reversed his position and changed course 180 degrees he took thousands with him that way, too.

Paul was so outstanding that he probably could have been a resounding success in any field he chose to enter. But God got to him and so captured him that he devoted himself to service in the Name of Christ, service that led him to great hardship and deprivation.

His was a voluntary subjection to the demands of Christ and the unpleasant temporal ramifications of that identification. He could have returned to his old life of prestige and acceptance by reconverting to what he had left. But that was unthinkable.

Paul had made a commitment of identification with Christ that led him to expect no better treatment than Christ had received; every deprivation which Paul suffered, though decidedly unpleasant, was nevertheless an evidence of his privileged position as "servant of Jesus Christ." The discipline of discomfort is part of Christian discipleship. It is not to be avoided or evaded, but accepted as part of the learning process.

The Discipline of Disappointment

Disappointment is one of those things that hits where it hurts most. To have your high hopes grounded and your bubbles burst is tough. Paul had more than his share of disappointment, not least his imprisonment, but he had learned that disappointment can be *His*-appointment.

It all depends which way you look at it.

When things don't work out the way you determine they ought to work out, disappointment can result. On the other hand, if you believe that things are working out as He determines, disappointment can only result if you find God disappointing and His will less than acceptable.

However, we must always remember that we have no right to call events in our lives "His appointments" if they are the products of our disobedience or the fruits of sin.

Willful sin can only produce awful disappointment, and settled disobedience will produce unsettling repercussions.

From the results of Paul's imprisonment, we can see that the disciplines of delay, discomfort and disappointment all happened according to God's plan for him. But there was something else happening to him at the same time. Perhaps it was even harder to take than his imprisonment. He explains in verse 16 that there are some people who were seeking "to add affliction to my bonds." As if chains were not enough, there were some supposed saints adding their special brand of opposition to Paul's suffering. They had seen his imprisonment as their opportunity to make things worse for him.

Paul always had his opponents. It was inevitable, simply because the Christian message is a very demanding and abrasive message. Some people tell me about their pastor, "He never had an enemy. Everybody loved him." I always feel, when I hear sentiment like that, either the people are living in a fool's paradise, or the pastor was doing something seriously wrong. Jesus had His enemies, so did Paul. And so does every servant of God who has a decisive and incisive message. And the only message he is authorized to bring has those characteristics.

Paul's problems at this time came from the Judaizers. They dogged his footsteps, confused his converts, wrecked his missions and generally tried to give him a hard time.

These were not the Jews who rejected Christ, or the Greeks who regarded the whole idea of Christ as "foolishness." Nor were they pagans of Corinth or Ephesus. They were professing Christians who were "preaching Christ."

I used to play Rugby football, a tough contact sport. For years I got by without any serious injury until one day I was hit by an illegal tackle and injured my collarbone. When you know that a tackle is coming you instinctively prepare for it, but when it comes from an unexpected quarter, there is no way that you can prepare and you inevitably get hurt.

That's how it was with Paul. He was accustomed to being hit by his opposition, but when his teammates started hitting him on the blind side, that was rough. He got hurt and hurt badly. If there was a time when he needed their love and prayer support, it was then. But instead of love, there was hate, and instead of desire to share his load, there was intent to add to it. Things certainly happened to him!

The Things That Happened to Me

If Paul had said no more, this would indeed have been a tale of woe. But we must be careful to see that he only raised the subject of "the things that happened *to* me" as an introduction to telling "the things that happened *in* me."

While he was sitting in prison with all these things going on, God was at work in his life helping him to get some very special perspectives on the situation. The importance of perspective in spiritual experience cannot be stressed too much.

Problems into Perspective

To be able to get problems into perspective is to be able to enjoy one of the greatest Christian graces. To be swamped by problems and overwhelmed by difficulties is relatively simple. Just stand there and they'll do the rest! But to get your overwhelming problems into perspective takes a work of the Spirit of God in your life.

Some people worship their problems more regularly and with greater fervor than they worship their Lord. They bow down to them, have their behavior governed by them and generally allow their lives to revolve around them.

Others ignore them. To them problems admitted as problems should not be part of the Christian's experience.

To have a problem is to be unspiritual, and to admit difficulty is tantamount to "defeat." If difficulties are defeats and defeats are unspiritual, then difficulties must be glossed over in the name of spirituality. A very strange thing results—hypocrisy is called spirituality.

God no more wants us to worship our problems than He wants us to ignore them and pretend we don't have them. As He allowed them to come, He can hardly be pleased with us if we ignore them or pretend they don't come! And as He gave permission for them, He can hardly be impressed with us if we worship that which He permitted more than He who did the permitting. He simply wants them in the right perspective.

The correct perspective comes through acknowledging God as the authorizer of the problem and through seeing that His authorization is a work of love designed to lead you into deeper knowledge of Him and greater usefulness for Him. Then the problem will be dealt with, not in mute acquiescence or resigned stoicism, but with alert anticipation and spiritual insight.

Pain into Perspective

In verse 18 Paul says, "What then? notwithstanding, every way, whether in pretense, or in truth, Christ is preached; and I therein do rejoice, yea, and will rejoice." That is a very big statement. It comes from a man deeply hurt personally and ideologically. But he has come to terms with his hurt so thoroughly that he can talk about rejoicing and going on rejoicing.

Paul did not arrive at this point overnight. Whatever we may think of Paul, he was no alabaster saint on a pedestal. The statue and the pedestal are the products of our own lack of reality. The real Paul had a temper that got heated and feelings that got hurt. He was no computerized theological machine churning out inspired writings, but a very warm human individual who needed as much love as the next man, and then some.

You can't hurt a computer's feelings or grieve a theological concept, but you can destroy a man. Paul was destructible, but he wasn't destroyed. And it wasn't for lack of somebody trying! The perspective that he had discovered allowed him to say that he didn't really mind what happened to him so long as nothing happened to stop the gospel, because in his understanding the message preached mattered more than the man preaching.

The church does not always give the impression that it believes this to be true. Personal feelings and prejudices are often allowed to take precedence over the effectiveness of evangelical witness.

Paul is hurt by the fact that these brethren reject some aspects of the gospel that he holds dear, but he has coped with that, too. He does not insist that they must dot his *i*'s and cross his *t*'s if they are to do the job. He admits that it is possible for Christ to be preached by people who disagree with him on some theological matters.

It's about time the present-day church got over some hurts in this area. Much conservative theology has been so carefully conserved that it has been kept from those who need it most. While those who have it give the impression that their main goal in life is to keep it, God in His heaven is looking for men and women who will get it out where it belongs.

The methods and the motives of Paul's opponents were less than satisfactory in Paul's eyes. But method and motive were not his prime concern. The message was. The conclusion we can draw from this is perfectly clear: message matters more than method.

Possibilities in Perspective

In verse 19 Paul says, "I know that this shall turn to my salvation through your prayer, and the supply of the Spirit of Jesus Christ." Now that's better than feeling sorry for himself and asking God, "What do you think you're doing?" Note the word "salvation," for by using it in this sense Paul is getting the *possibilities of salvation into perspective*. He is not talking about initial salvation from sin's consequences. He's talking about the salvation that he needs to experience in prison, which is presumably salvation from fear and frustration and related subjects.

Evangelical Christians in their evangelism make much of the message of salvation as it relates to man's eternal destiny and spiritual welfare. Quite rightly so. But there are facets of salvation that have nothing to do with a coming day but everything to do with the days that have come.

As the days followed each other in monotonous, relentless order for Paul, I feel sure that he knew fear and frustration. He didn't need saving from the temptation to fornication, for obvious reasons, but he did need saving from the temptation to frustration. Self-indulgence would be no problem on a prison diet, but self-pity would be a massive problem. Paul's prison gives him the chance to experience new areas of salvation because it leads him into new areas of need.

Then he has the opportunity to get the *possibilities of sufficiency into perspective*. Perhaps one of the greatest statements to come from the lips of Paul was, "For to me to live is Christ, and to die is gain" (v. 21). He meant by this statement that Christ was not only *his reason for living*, but also his *resource for living*. Reasons and resource combined in Christ to make Him the focal point of Paul's existence and the enabling dynamic of his life.

It is not uncommon to find people without a reason for living. They simply exist until they can bear it no longer, or they fill their empty hopelessness with meaningless pursuits. Other people have reason to live without the resource to live. Their reason for living when attained leaves them sadly disappointed or strangely empty. Not so Paul. He has both in Christ.

Christ is Paul's reason for living because He is Lord. Christ is Paul's beginning and his end, his origin and his destiny. Christ is his creator and his judge. Without Christ he has come from nowhere and is headed straight back. But with Christ he knows whence he came and he knows where he is going. Christ has the undisputed right to order circumstances, dictate terms, make demands and expect results. Christ is Paul's reason for living.

More than that, however, Christ is Paul's resource for living. "Through the supply of the Spirit of Jesus Christ" the living Lord Jesus has entered Paul's life as surely as Paul's body has entered the cell. Christ through His Spirit is as alive in Paul as Paul is alive in his cell. In the same way that the presence of Paul is evident in the cell through the actions of his body and the projections of his personality, so Christ in all His risen power is active in Paul. The projections of the personality of Christ are going to be evidence that there is no situation in that cell or any other cell that is greater than the sufficiency of Christ who is Paul's life.

It is not hard to imagine the confidence that this produced in Paul even at his worst moments. Nothing too great for the living Lord could come his way. Nothing outside the will of God could cross his path. There are many people in our world today who would give their right arms for a philosophy of life that would give them this kind of sufficiency and confidence. For the great difficulty that so many people experience is the difficulty of learning to cope with situations that are too big for them.

There was also the shadow of an executioner constantly falling across the entrance to Paul's cell. So he had to do more than prepare for the eventualities of life. He had to come up with some answers for death as well. While life is full of possibilities, death is full of certainty. It is ironic that the only certainty in life is death. Most people don't like to admit it, but they should. Insurance men don't like to admit it in their sales pitch. "If something should happen to you . . . " is their line. I told one of them not to say that to me because it upset me. He said I shouldn't be upset about the possibility of death, and I told him I wasn't upset with the possibility, I was upset that he didn't seem to realize it was a certainty.

Funeral directors are highly skilled at taking our minds off the inevitability of death to such a degree that when it finally happens they work hard to make everybody think it hasn't happened. When they're through, some people look better in death than they did in life.

Paul was as realistic about death as he was about life. "To die is gain," is how he explained his attitude to the inevitable. These were not noble words or brave rhetoric. They were the solemn words of a realist who had often locked horns with death, only to be delivered because God wasn't through with him. But he was fairly certain that his days were numbered, and he was awaiting the time of his departure with superb equanimity.

Death to Paul was not the ultimate tragedy. It was the entrance into unbelievable glory. In his mind death was the brief intermission between act one and act two of the story of his existence. Act one had been great because Christ was the reason and resource for it. But act two would be better yet: Christ would still be the reason and resource for it, but the unpleasant things like shipwrecks and whippings and prisons and nasty Christians would not bother him any more. As far as Paul was concerned, life including these things and Christ had been great; therefore, life including Christ, but excluding these things, had to be better. What great things had been happening in Paul!

The Things That Happened Through Me

Nobody knew better than Paul that the things happening in him were not happening solely for his benefit. They were happening *in* him so that things would happen *through* him.

One of the initial results of his imprisonment is what Paul calls the "furtherance of the gospel" (v. 12).

New Areas Were Pioneered

It is fascinating to see how God works in mysterious ways. He wanted to reach the people in the palace, or "Praetorium," which can mean either Caesar's court or his bodyguard.

How did God go about reaching this select group? He did not get a fine young Christian man to be a soldier in the bodyguard, or a beautiful young Christian girl to be a member of the court. Instead, He put Paul in prison and sent soldiers to guard him. They took turns of duty, and, no doubt, found that they had inadvertently enrolled in a course of systematic theology. At the end of each turn of duty (or lesson) one team of soldiers were relieved by more soldiers (or students), and as time went on the work of infiltration was done. All over the Praetorium the talk was of Paul and his gospel. That's one way of pioneering new areas!

New People Were Mobilized

As a result of Paul's experience new people were mobilized. Some of Paul's contemporaries were like some of the Lord's people today. They lacked confidence in their testimony. But when they saw Paul doing what he did best they "waxed confident" and presumably came to the conclusion that if he could do it "inside," they could certainly do it "outside." So more people were mobilized. Unfortunately the work of the church is often left by the majority to the overworked minority. The followers are most happy to leave it to the leaders. God deals with this kind of situation in various ways, but one of the most drastic is to take away the leadership. It usually works beautifully, as it did in this case.

We must not minimize the dangers of a virile ministry in Paul's day. It is not surprising that many of the Christians were a little reluctant to open their mouths too wide for fear they would end up with their heads inside a lion's mouth. Despite this threat to their well-being, there were those who overcame their fears and became "much more bold to speak the word without fear."

New Victories Were Won

Veterans are of great value to rookies if they help rather than criticize them. Many an athlete has been able to conquer his "butterflies" on the big occasion simply because an old-timer gave him the right word at the right time. That was the effect that Paul was having on the Christians.

New Glories Were Seen

New glories were seen, for Christ was being "magnified" in Paul's body. Paul's circumstances were beyond a man's capabilities, but he came through quite capably. The reason was Christ in his life. The degree in which Paul did what he couldn't, and was what he wasn't, was the degree in which Christ was magnified.

Christians who are content to do what they can, must be content to magnify their own abilities in their lives. Those who want to magnify Christ must expect to be taken to the edge of their abilities so that they must draw upon the untapped resources which are theirs in Christ.

Questions for Discussion

1. How has God used the "discipline of delay" to accomplish His will in your life? How would your life be different today if there had not been a delay?

2. How can you reconcile the "discipline of disappointment" with verses like Romans 8:28; Matthew 7:7; and John 15:7?

3. In what ways has today's church become like the Judaizers of Paul's day? How do we emphasize outward evidence of belief over the inward?

4. What is the greatest problem you face today? How does it look when put in the perspective of God's sovereign control on your life?

3
WATCH YOUR CONDUCT

Only let your conversation be as it becometh the gospel of Christ: that whether I come and see you, or else be absent, I may hear of your affairs, that ye stand fast in one spirit, with one mind striving together for the faith of the gospel; and in nothing terrified by your adversaries: which is to them an evident token of perdition, but to you of salvation, and that of God. For unto you it is given in the behalf of Christ, not only to believe on him, but also to suffer for his sake; having the same conflict which ye saw in me, and now hear to be in me.

Philippians 1:27-30

So far in our study of Philippians we have been dealing mainly with autobiographical passages which have shown us Paul with the lid off. As he is one of the most exciting and exhilarating Christians who has ever lived, it is beneficial to study what made him tick, as an encouragement and challenge to our own spiritual experience.

God does not want us to be little apostle Pauls, but He does require us to put into practice the principles that Paul learned and taught in order that we might be as effective in our generation as Paul was in his.

Beginning with verse 27, however, Paul changes gears. Instead of speaking about his own experience he starts to speak to the Philippians about theirs. The thrust of his concern is that they should be careful of their lifestyle and watch their conduct. In order to understand clearly the content of these verses, we should notice three important considerations.

The Challenge of Christian Conduct

"Only let your conversation be as it becometh the gospel of Christ" (v. 27). We use the word "conversation" to mean a situation where people are talking. When the King James edition was translated, however, "conversation" had a different connotation. It meant "conduct, way of life or behavior pattern," and that is what is meant in verse 27. In fact, the Greek word translated "conversation" is the word from which we get our words "politics" and "police," and has to do with the idea of citizenship. So the concern that Paul expresses is related to their behavior as citizens.

"Becometh" is another important word. It means "to be of equal weight," and so we can paraphrase these words by saying, "Make sure that your behavior as citizens adds up to the gospel you present." Therein lies the challenge of Christian behavior.

Be Consistent in All Areas

As we have already seen, Christian behavior is related to citizenship. Perhaps it would be true to say that Christians have a tendency to divorce their spiritual convictions from their citizenship behavior. Yet the Christian should be true to the principles of the gospel of Christ in all areas of citizenship. To think this through is to present yourself with some big questions that need some big answers.

A young man came up to me one day and asked me, "Is it possible to be a Christian on the freeway in rush hour?" I laughed until I saw that he was not laughing. He was serious. I had to admit that I had never thought about it because I had driven on the freeways according to the generally accepted rule of "the survival of the fittest." But the gospel is not a gospel of the survival of the fittest, it is a gospel of the fittest serving and caring for the weakest. Try translating that into freeway driving next time you are returning home in the rush hour. But keep your eye on the road while you're thinking it through!

There are people in business who will tell you quite bluntly that it is impossible to run a business on Christian principles. So they have decided that it is perfectly all right for them to function according to the gospel on Sundays, to jump into the business jungle Mondays through Fridays and to vegetate on Saturdays. But this is not tenable according to the Scriptures. I was a businessman for a number of years before entering the ministry, and I know that it is no easy matter for a businessman in this day and age to be consistent. But who's interested in doing only what's easy?

Because of a consistency breakdown in these and other areas, the church has been a "sitting duck" for many of its critics, and because of this, the message of the gospel of Christ has suffered.

There is little point talking about consistency if we do not define clearly the standard with which we are expected to be consistent. Paul is quite clear on this point. He doesn't say, "Be consistent"; he says, "Be consistent with the gospel of Christ." Think of the gospel for a minute. What are its characteristics?

It is a *gospel of love,* so if you are consistent you will be loving. There is no point identifying with a church that preaches love from the pulpit if you are not going to project love in the parking lot! Don't give a man a tract telling him of the love of God if you can't bring yourself to love him as a brother after he has believed the message of your tract.

It is a *gospel of life,* so if you are consistent you will not have a boring life-style and a dull personality. If you present a gospel that tells a woman that she can be the recipient of life eternal today, but you live as if you have only experienced acid indigestion, you are hardly consistent. Eternal life is unique and classy, and people who enjoy it have a touch of class about their lives that is not found in the unredeemed.

It is the *gospel of liberty,* so if you are consistent you will not be strung out with hang-ups. The watching world doesn't want to hear you thunder liberty from the pulpit while clanking the chains of prejudice and fear from your evangelical ankles. A gospel of liberty deserves better advertising than it gets in much of our daily living.

Persistent at All Times

Paul says, "Whether I come and see you, or else be absent, I may hear of your affairs . . . " (v. 27). Evidently, the Philippians were conscious of dignitaries, and Paul had his suspicion that they were. He seemed to think that they might behave one way if he were there and be themselves when he wasn't there. It's a common human failing.

When I was an English Royal Marine the king came to visit the city where I was stationed. Much labor and money were expended on polishing up areas of the city that the king would traverse on his carefully chosen route.

The marines were required to line the route. We were up all night preparing our full dress uniforms, then were transported to our positions and stood for hours in the pouring rain. And the king simply drove past in his limousine. He didn't even look in my direction! Maybe he wasn't very interested, or perhaps he knew that the whole thing was not normal, it was a special display put on for his benefit, and he wasn't very impressed. I felt sorry for him living his life being subjected to carefully prepared spectacles somewhat removed from reality.

There is no doubt that it is sometimes easier to be on your toes if a celebrity is around, or to act in a consistent way if you know that you're being watched. But to be persistent at all times is hard, and that is the challenge of Christian conduct.

One night my wife took some friends on an outreach escapade into one of our famous English pubs. Once inside, two or three of them got into conversation with some fine, clean-cut, all-American boys who were sitting in a corner quietly drinking their beer. It transpired that they were Mormon missionaries (Clean-cut American young people in out-of-the-way areas of England usually are Mormon missionaries!)

One of the people with my wife said, somewhat rudely, "I thought Mormons didn't drink coffee or tea or take drugs or alcohol."

To which the young missionaries replied, "That's right, but even missionaries need a break once in a while!"

That I would not deny, but if the "break" is a breakdown in consistency, it poses severe problems.

The Characteristics of Christian Conduct

Having insisted that we should be consistent and persistent, Paul goes on to say, "that . . . I may hear of your affairs, that ye stand fast . . . " (v. 27). Here we find three characteristics that Paul looks for.

Faithfulness

The blessed ability to hold your ground, to see a thing through, to be reliable and responsible. Character that shows stickability is impressive to even the most severe critic. Unfortunately, it is not as common as might reasonably be expected.

One of my favorite chapters of the Bible is 2 Samuel 23. It tells a number of stories concerning David's right hand men. They were a fascinating group, particularly when you remember that when David first got his hands on them they were the dregs of society. But he made them into reliable, faithful men. Adino found himself up against 800 at one time and saw the job through. His colleague Eleazar had such a day in the field on one occasion that they had to take his sword out of his hand, one finger at a time, because his hand was so tired and numb he couldn't release it himself.

My favorite is Benaiah, who had a hard day. Everything went wrong. Whenever I have a hard day, I think of my friend Benaiah. When he started off the day he found it was snowing. That is enough to make many people quit! But he kept going, and killed two "lion-like men of Moab" (v. 20). Then he fell in a pit. Even that wasn't enough: he had company in the pit—a lion! So he killed the lion too.

These men of David were faithful men who stood fast. It is this sort of attitude that Paul looks for in the people to whom he is writing.

Forcefulness

"Stand fast in one spirit, with one mind striving together for the faith of the gospel." Our popular word "athletics" derives from the Greek word that is translated "striving together."

Athletics includes many things today, but in its original

use the word had to do with wrestling. Not modern wrestling, but team wrestling. The competing teams would line up facing each other, with each team member shoulder to shoulder with his colleague and facing his opponent. At a given signal both teams would leap into action and soon there would be one great sweating, writhing, wrestling mass of humanity. "Wrestling together," Paul calls it, and says that Christian conduct should bear some resemblance in its efforts for the faith of the gospel.

I find it helpful to be reminded that being a Christian has striking similarities to the life of the trained athlete, and that Christian behavior demands considerable output of what Winston Churchill called "blood, sweat and tears." We need challenges to keep us fresh, and new exposure to pressure and demand to keep us alive. There is no shortage of demand and pressure in the challenge to forceful conduct.

Some people are bewildered by a seeming contradiction in Scripture. We have forcefulness on one hand with images of athletic competition and military discipline. On the other hand, the Bible speaks of the "rest of faith," "abiding in Christ," and similar terms.

There is no conflict, however. The terms that speak of rest and trust relate to the inner attitude that the believer has toward the indwelling Lord who is the source of strength and sufficiency. The wrestling and the fighting have to do with the outcome of this relationship in terms of the believer's encounter with the forces of evil as they confront his own life and wreck the lives of those whom he desires to reach for Christ.

Christian conduct includes both rest and wrestling. It joyfully marries sweet faith and sweaty fighting. Without the rest and trust that release the power of Christ there will be no effective grappling with spiritual conduct. But real rest and faith demonstrate themselves in vigorous activity.

Before we leave the wrestling, there is one more thing we should note. Paul wants the believers' wrestling to be shoulder to shoulder and "with one mind." Beware of this word "mind." It does not mean that so long as you give mental assent to the necessity of forceful living that is all that is asked of you. "Mind" is really "soul." In other words, put your heart and soul into your behavior. A little bit of enthusiasm goes a long way!

Fearlessness

"And in nothing terrified by your adversaries" (Phil 1:28). Paul's word for "terrified" is graphic. It is the word that was used to describe a horse shying when it is frightened.

When I was in high school it was announced one day that a volunteer was needed to drive a horse and cart full of equipment to a stadium across town where an athletic meeting was going to be held. I knew absolutely nothing about a horse and cart. But I didn't let a little thing like that deter me. My major concern was to miss a morning of lessons.

With much help I got the horse between the shafts and with a whack of the reins I set off in the right direction. All went well until the horse saw a donkey. It was terrified, reared on its hind legs, threw me from my precarious perch and took off down the road. There was little cart left when the horse was finally brought under control three miles away. There is nothing quite so frightening as a frightened horse.

Horses are easily frightened and so are Christians. They both upset the cart when they shy away from something. Paul says to his friends in Philippi, "Don't shy away from your opponents." He knew, of course, that they had plenty. There were the Romans who were edgy about the Christians from a political point of view. Then there were

the Philippian unbelievers who had given Paul rough treatment. They hadn't changed much. On top of that there
was trouble from the people who disagreed with Paul's
theology. And, to round off the full array of people who
were making things difficult, there were Euodias and Syntyche. From every angle there was trouble.

Paul's instruction to the believers is, "don't shy away,"
for fearlessness is an integral part of mature conduct. Conduct always affects other people. Paul is keenly aware of
this, for he states that their fearlessness is an "evident
token of perdition" to all their adversaries.

There are some who say that this phrase refers to the
days of the great Roman spectacles when the vast crowds
gathered in the Colosseum and the Circus Maximus to
watch the violent sporting activities. One of the most popular events was the gladiatorial combat in which two men
would fight until one had overcome the other. As the
defeated man lay on the sand with his victor standing over
him, a great hush would fall on the crowd and every eye
would turn to Caesar sitting on his dais. Caesar would
then give a sign for all to see. If he felt the gladiator had
acquitted himself well, even though he had been defeated,
he gave the "thumbs up" which meant "let him go." If Caesar was displeased with the gladiator's performance, he
gave the "thumbs down" and the man was killed. Paul may
well have had this in mind when he said fearless Christian
living is an "evident token," for it gives the "thumbs up"
sign to some and the "thumbs down" to others.

The adversaries get the thumbs-down sign from God
when they see a Christian who refuses to be afraid even
when he has good reason to be afraid. Such a Christian is a
living example of what God can do in a life, and that is a
great condemnation to a person who is antagonistic to God
and His work.

A Christian in school can give the thumbs-down sign to
a bully by refusing to back off when the bully takes issue

with the Christian's position. There is nothing that makes a bully look more foolish than someone who isn't afraid of his bullying tactics.

Business people can soon bring condemnation of crooked business practice by the simple expedient of being straight, even though the consequences may well be harmful for them. Faithfulness, forcefulness and fearlessness are the characteristics for which Paul is looking.

The Cost of Christian Conduct

Christian conduct can be, and often is, a costly activity. Verse 29 banishes any misconceptions that there may be on this point: "For unto you it is given in the behalf of Christ, not only to believe on him, but also to suffer for his sake."

There are treasures of truth that we may miss in this verse. "Given" is a word that means "a gift of grace." We are all well acquainted with the grace of God and the way it has worked on our behalf, making it possible for us to believe and be saved. But were you aware that the gift of grace is not only to believe, but also to suffer? Suffering is as much a gracious provision of a gracious God as the opportunity to believe.

The reason is that while belief produces spiritual life, suffering produces spiritual muscles. God's gift of grace is the muscle-building equipment that people call suffering. When we have it easy, we also get flabby, but when we have it hard, we tend to grow up tough.

Dull Christianity can easily be produced in a comfortable pew. It requires nothing more than faithful sitting and diligent ignoring of the challenges of the Word. But, once the challenges of the Word are accepted, the toughness starts and the dullness goes.

I have seen countless examples of churches full of unchallenged, unmotivated, unpalatable saints doing little but putting in time till the Millennium. I've seen these same people revolutionized because they began to act on what they believed, got out where the action is, took some knocks and grew beyond all recognition.

Suffering is God's precious gift to us. Don't miss it. Don't think, however, that I am suggesting that you should go out and start looking for trouble. That will not be necessary. Just do what God expects a recipient of grace to do, and the trouble will come looking for you.

Some time ago I visited a young couple who wanted to commit their lives to Christ, but the wife had a problem. She told me that it had taken her about five years to get in to the local bridge and cocktail circle, and she was a little concerned that her Christian position might pose some problems. I told her that there was no doubt it would, but she shouldn't worry about it. She should just go ahead and share with them what she had discovered. She suffered, but she also won. Her group, after its initial dismay and chagrin at her conversion, saw the difference in her life. She changed her group more than her group changed her. But it was rough going.

There is no quick trip to maturity, and there is no instant recipe for growth, but there are principles for behavior. When they are followed, growth and maturity have a habit of coming right along. So watch your behavior.

Questions for Discussion

1. What are the outward signs of American citizenship? What responsibilities go with the privileges of citizenship? How are these characteristics applicable to our heavenly citizenship?

2. How does the gospel of love, life, and liberty find manifestation in your daily life?

3. How can you "give yourself a break" and not experience a "breakdown" in consistency?

4. In what ways does your Christian life compare to the life of an athlete in training? What areas need to be shaped up?

5. How has suffering been a gift from God in your life? What is the difference between suffering as a means of identifying with Christ and buffetings sent from Satan?

4
HOW TO GET ALONG WITH CHRISTIANS

If there be therefore any consolation in Christ, if any comfort of love, if any fellowship of the Spirit, if any bowels and mercies, fulfill ye my joy, that ye be likeminded, having the same love, being of one accord, of one mind. Let nothing be done through strife or vainglory; but in lowliness of mind let each esteem other better than themselves. Look not every man on his own things, but every man also on the things of others.

Philippians 2:1-4

We Christians seem to have a hard time learning from the mistakes of the past, for the same old things keep on happening. One area where this is obvious is that of interpersonal relationships among Christians. There are encouraging signs of improvement at the present time, but there is need for much more.

Perhaps the problem is caused partially by our failure to realize how crucial is the need for correct relationships. The Lord stipulated the basis upon which Christian testimony would become viable in the eyes of the watching world. "By this shall all men know that ye are my disciples, if ye have love one to another" (John 13:35). Christ said quite bluntly that the thing that will give credibility to the message of God's love is the evidence of the love of God in the messengers. If God's people don't love one another, how are the unreached going to be reached with God's love?

Besides obscuring the evangelistic message, inter-Christian strife dissipates the energies of Christians. It diverts them from the real object of their warfare: Satan and his cohorts. To a large extent the effectiveness of a body of believers in thwarting the designs of Satan is directly related to that body's effectiveness in fighting itself. There is only so much nervous and physical energy in all of us, and the more we expend in fighting each other, the less there will be for the real task to which we have been called.

On the other hand, the more we fight the real enemy, the more we'll gladly accept the help and fellowship of all who will identify with us. It is clearly a case of knowing your enemy!

With these things in mind, let's see what the Scriptures have to say on the subject. First, there is a clear indication that getting along with Christians has to be closely related to understanding them. To understand a Christian it is necessary to understand what he believes.

Remember Doctrinal Facts

I realize that when you are nose to nose with a heated saint you may have neither the desire nor the ability to concentrate on doctrine at that moment. But wait a minute!

Consolation in Christ

It is surely not necessary to say that every Christian has a personal relationship with Christ, but it is necessary to remember it when discord develops. For the people between whom the discord arises are both members of Christ, and, therefore, any damage inflicted by one on the other is really self-destructive. Hands and teeth usually get along well together, particularly if they belong to the same body. Hands have been known to punch teeth, and teeth have been known to bite hands, but rarely on the same body. That is what happens when Christians fight each other. They bite their own hands and punch their own teeth, for they, in Christ, are members "one of the other."

Comfort of Love

Love purportedly makes the world go 'round, but if it does it isn't human love. It is divine love, the great motivating factor of the universe, which is entirely responsible for the existence of mankind and also for our redemption and reconciliation to a holy God.

Any redeemed soul and reconciled life, any recycled person that you meet, is in that condition because he understands something of the love of God and has responded to that which he knows. Love is at the root of his experience. Christians know this better than anyone, but choose to forget it in the heat of the moment. When Christians remember God's love at a moment of crisis, they realize how foolish it is to allow hostility to exist between people whose existence, standing and survival are totally dependent upon love.

Fellowship of the Spirit

Scripture says, "If any man have not the Spirit of Christ, he is none of his" (Rom. 8:9). So we can see that if a person *does* belong to Christ, he *does* have the Spirit of Christ indwelling him.

Now the Spirit of Christ is known to be a mortal foe of all that savors of selfishness and egotism. How then is it possible for two Christians, who by definition are indwelt by the same Spirit who is totally opposed to selfishness, to get into a fight that is evidence of their own hard-hearted and unyielding nature? Only by discounting the Spirit and forgetting their doctrine!

Exposure to Spiritual Influences

Secondly, we note that Christians get along with each other when they are exposed to spiritual influences.

If you have your three doctrinal facts carefully figured out, you should be ready for four spiritual influences.

The Encouraging Influence of Christ

"Consolation" is usually reserved for bereaved people or runners-up in beauty pageants. But there is much more to it than the connotation of pity that these uses evoke. The Greek word has the meaning of someone standing with you and being an encouragement to you.

I spoke to a group of German young people once. There was a little problem, though, because I knew no German, and their English was equally deficient. But there was a great encouragement beside me: my interpreter.

The knowledge of the presence of Christ in His capacity as Encourager is a great influence on the life of a believer. He encourages you to find solutions instead of taking sides. He encourages you to be as patient with others as He is with you. He encourages humility and sacrifice, and will always encourage us all to peace and reconciliation. This encouragement comes from His example which is clearly delineated in the Gospels, and through His enabling which is readily available through His Spirit.

The Softening Influence of Love

Those of us who are married know that when our spouses get home in the evening, tired from the day at the office, irritated from the drive on the freeway, cold because the car heater broke, and worried over a possible transfer, they are one kind of people. We also know that a warm shower, a good meal, and a little tender loving care will make new people out of them . . . . Then they would recall that the other person is loved, too, by God if not by them.

A friend of mine struck me with a simple observation recently. He said, "I've come to the conclusion that nobody really wants to be nasty and hateful and unpleasant, and if they are like that they must have a problem." I'm sure he is right, and I'm equally sure that understanding this will make it easier to love instead of fighting. It's not too hard to fight someone who you think is being unpleasant, but you can't feel good about making things more difficult for a person with a difficulty!

The Unifying Influence of the Spirit

"Fellowship" is a favorite word in the ecclesiastical vocabulary. It can mean anything from coffee and cake in a church basement to softball at the annual picnic. But it should mean much more in the life of a believer than socializing. One basic Greek word is translated by the English words, "common, communion, fellowship," and the idea is simply "sharing."

When the Christians in Jerusalem had "all things in

common" they shared everything. When the Corinthians had "communion" they shared the bread and the wine in common remembrance of the risen Lord. Fellowship is one of the most beautiful privileges and graces of the Christian experience, for it lifts a person out of his isolation and introduces him into a life of caring and sharing.

This works two ways. When two Christians are in fellowship with one another, and one is in need, his needs will be met if the other can meet them. Later the tables might be turned. It is beautiful to see brethren living under the unifying, sharing, caring influence of the Spirit.

The Breaking Influence of Mercy

There are three words that are occasionally confused in people's minds: the words *justice, mercy* and *grace.* They are all related, but they are not to be confused. *Justice* makes sure that people get what they deserve. *Grace* gives them what they don't deserve. *Mercy* doesn't give people all that they do deserve.

Suppose a father finds it necessary to discipline his son. He should make sure that he deals firmly with the boy on the basis of justice. Say, five whacks with the board of education on the seat of learning! After the administration of four whacks of justice, the father may choose to omit one whack. That's mercy! Then he may feel that his boy, bruised and battered, needs a little encouragement, so he gives him an ice cream. That's grace!

God deals with man on the basis of justice in judging his sin as He is committed to do. But He judged that sin in Christ, the perfect atonement for sin, and that was the demonstration of grace that will never be surpassed.

Then, on top of that, God has forgiven us constantly. He has been patient with us continually. He has protected us from the consequences of our own folly and sheltered us from the results of our stupidity. And that is mercy.

When a person understands justice, grace and mercy,

it tends to break him up. As he realizes the overwhelming goodness of God he is shattered by it all. Like John Whitfield standing one day by the gallows, he says, "There but for the grace of God go I." He bows his head and acknowledges the goodness and forbearance of God. Then he lifts his head and sees a man whom he has not forgiven in mercy. What does he do? With a heart shattered by mercy, he is merciful, and his brother may be in for a shock!

The influences that encourage and soften and unify and break are the influences that must never be resisted in the believer's life; and only if they are resisted will there be friction between Christians.

Attention to Personal Action

It isn't enough to be aware of doctrine or alert to influence. We must *act*.

A quick glance through the Scripture before us will show a series of imperatives. These imperatives are to be obeyed, not just underlined. An integral part of Christian belief is obedience. It isn't good enough for a Christian to give mental assent to doctrine or to demonstrate misty-eyed response to spiritual influences, if he does not obey God's commands. The major cause of conflict among Christians is not ignorance of doctrine or insensitivity to spiritual influence, but unwillingness to obey.

People sometimes fail to do what they are supposed to do because they have not been taught *what* to do or *how* to do it. If people are exposed to vague teaching, they may be strongly moved, but they will not know what action to take. So we must be quite clear on the course of action required.

Live Unitedly with Each Other

Paul says, "Be likeminded, having the same love, being of one accord, of one mind" (v. 2). These phrases are full of meaning, but it is obvious that the overriding theme is unity of mind and motive. Paul has already mentioned this, but he evidently thought it was necessary to repeat it.

Have you ever been troubled by your glaring failure to live in unity? Have you been tempted to say, "How on earth can we be expected to think alike and act alike when we are all so different?" Let's face it, however much we talk about unity, Christians can't even agree on the lengths of skirts, hair and sermons! In fact, they don't think the same thing about most things.

Are we then talking about something beautifully idealistic and thoroughly unrealistic? I don't believe so. Rather I am convinced that we misunderstand something fundamental about the biblical meaning of unity. To mind (or think) the same thing does not mean that all sense of individual thinking is put out of gear so that the "party line" might be superimposed, but rather that all individuals have their thinking molded by the impact of the Spirit. The Spirit leaves lots of elbow room for variety of thought and input.

When you attend a symphony concert you don't hear a stage full of people all playing the same note. Neither are they all playing their own separate compositions. Rather they are all scraping, banging, and blowing different parts clearly defined in the score under the direction of the conductor. And the result is not unison, but harmony.

To live unitedly requires a knowledge of your part of the score, respectful submission to the conductor and appreciation for the part played by the others in the orchestra. Your score is the Word of God. The conductor is the Holy Spirit, and the rest of the orchestra are your fellow believers. So if you haven't done it before, check to see if you are scraping your fiddle in harmony or just blowing your own trumpet to the intense irritation of all within earshot.

Behave Maturely to Each Other

"Let nothing be done through strife or vainglory" (v. 3). Here Paul talks about two serious causes of conflict among Christians. *Strife* means *party spirit* and *vainglory* means *empty pride*.

Some of the things that happened in Corinth were the product of *party spirit*. The fellowship had degenerated into factions. There were "Paul people" and "Apollos people" and "Peter people," and the really pious ones were the "Christ people." Instead of being united in Christ, they were fragmented by personalities.

No doubt some had been helped more by Paul than by Peter, and others were more compatible temperamentally with Apollos than with Paul, and so their affinity with some more than others was perfectly valid and understandable. But this was no cause for a campaign to boost their man and defeat the other.

We have the same kind of situation today. The "personality cult" is a fact of secular life. But it is dangerously evident in the Christian world, too. We have our personalities, and they have their followers. All this may be fine, but fighting over it isn't! It is great to be thrilled by someone so long as you are not threatened by a different person. But if we promote the one who thrills and attack the one who threatens, conflict and confusion will result.

Then there is the *empty pride* problem. Most actions produce reactions; and if the action is uncomplimentary or disappointing, the reaction may well be born of pride. This will only trigger more action that will give birth to more reactions, and so on *ad infinitum*. Somebody needs to blow the whistle somewhere along the line. Paul says who should blow it and when it should be blown. Those who are tempted to act or react from empty pride should refuse to do so, and they should make this refusal when the temptation comes . . . . So the passed-over prima donna walks out of the choir, with friends in tow. Now this is sometimes called "artistic temperament" and is good for publicity when it happens at the "Met" or La Scala, but it is called *empty pride* in the Scriptures and has no place in the church.

Relate Humbly to Each Other

"In lowliness of mind let each esteem the other better than themselves" (v. 3). Now this one poses some real problems. Does it mean that everybody must look on those who are less capable as if they are more capable? Do Ph.D.'s have to defer to sophomores, and elders to novices, and parents to children, and generals to sergeants? Not at all, because that is totally unrealistic and contrary to all biblical teaching of authority.

It does mean that everybody should be more interested in promoting others, encouraging others and caring for others than for himself. It means that we should so relate to others that we are considerably more "others-centered" than "self-centered."

Practically this is hard to do, but let me share something that I have found helpful. Try concentrating on the other person's good points and on your own bad points. This is contrary to nature, but in accord with the Scripture. Look at it this way: if your bad points are better than his good points, you must be almost ready for glory, and he is ready for lots of help. So you, being so close to glory, are the obvious person to give him the help he needs. On the other hand, if his good points are better than your bad points, he could conceivably have something to teach you.

Act Sacrificially for Each Other

"Look not every man on his own things, but every man also on the things of others. Let this mind be in you, which was also in Christ Jesus . . . " (vv. 4,5).

The greatest spur to Christian relationships is the one just mentioned, the attitude of our Lord Jesus. He did not "look . . . on his own things," but gazed with love and heartbreak "on the things of others." His own things were a throne and a crown, a position and a Name. But the things that He saw in the lives of men and women were sin and sorrow, disease and desperation. So He acted sacrificially by refusing to hold on to His rights, by exchanging His throne for a stable and His crown for a cross. And therein lies not only the basis of our redemption, but the principle of our behavior. For it was sacrifice that brought atonement to our souls, and it is sacrifice in life-style that brings liberty to our lives.

The Christian who needs to re-evaluate his thinking is the Christian who demands the sacrifice of Christ for his sins, but rejects the sacrificial attitude of Christ in his own life—in the nitty-gritty of personal relationships with people in general and Christians in particular. The servant is not greater than his Master, and sacrifice was His method and it must be ours.

So there we have some straightforward instructions on how to get along with Christians. They are superlative and challenging and possible through the obedience of submissive lives and the power of the indwelling Spirit.

Questions for Discussion

1. What is the essence of true fellowship? How can it be made a more integral part of the activities of your church?

2. In what ways are Christians today called to have all things in common?

3. Can you find Scriptures to match the author's definitions of *justice, grace,* and *mercy?*

4. Is it possible for a congregation to be like-minded and yet remain individuals? How can unity and diversity co-exist?

5. In what ways does the church today exalt its leaders over the supremacy of Christ and the fellowship of believers? How can the church combat such misplaced pride?

5

CHRIST SUPREME

Let this mind be in you, which was also in Christ Jesus: who, being in the form of God, thought it not robbery to be equal with God: but made himself of no reputation, and took upon him the form of a servant, and was made in the likeness of men: and being found in fashion as a man, he humbled himself, and became obedient unto death, even the death of the cross. Wherefore God also hath highly exalted him, and given him a name which is above every name: that at the name of Jesus every knee should bow, of things in heaven, and things in earth, and things under the earth; and that every tongue should confess that Jesus Christ is Lord, to the glory of God the Father.

Philippians 2:5-11

The church of Jesus Christ has only one message—to preach Christ. You wouldn't always get that impression, but that's how it ought to be. There are so many aspects of who the Lord Jesus is, and what He says, and what He did and what He teaches and what He requires and how we can know Him and what we can do about it—there are so many different things to know that it can keep you going for the whole of the ministry simply preaching Christ. And even in a whole lifetime you will never exhaust all that there is to know about Christ.

One of the Scriptures that gives a summary of who Christ is and what He did is Philippians 2:5-11. This is what the theologians would call one of the outstanding Christological passages. It is one of the lovely places where we see Jesus exalted and demonstrated to be the Lord that He really is.

Before we look into this passage of Christ Supreme I want you to notice first of all why it was written. It wasn't written just as a theological treatise on the person of Christ, and it wasn't written to be an outstanding Christological passage—it was actually written as an illustration of the attitude that ought to govern a person who professes to be a Christian. So the whole passage is introduced in verse 5 with these words: "Let this mind [or attitude] be in you, which was also in Christ Jesus."

Paul had been talking to the Philippian Christians about how to get along with Christians and how to enjoy fellowship and what to do about certain situations. Having outlined all that, he then wrote this tremendous passage which summarizes the whole thing. He said, "Now listen, have the attitude of Christ in your life." And then he started off to explain the attitude of Christ as it was seen in His life. Paul got carried away with this theme, and he didn't really land for about six or seven verses. Let's join Paul and allow ourselves to be caught up with who Christ is in all His supremacy.

Christis Supreme in Being

The first thing that I want you to notice is this—that Christ is supreme in being. Verse 6 says that Christ was "in the form of God." The word *form* means literally that He outwardly manifested the inner reality of His being. And the statement is quite straightforward that Christ's inner reality was *deity*.

Too many people want to reject the deity of the Lord Jesus in these days. They will say many lovely things about Him, and they will say many true things about Him, but they deny the basic fact that Jesus Christ is the Son of God.

People run into problems over the Trinity. Because they can't understand the Trinity they deny the existence of the Trinity. Because they haven't come across anything like the Trinity in any other form, they deny the possibility of a Trinity in divine form.

But their argument doesn't hold together. If God is God, He is Supreme; and if God is Supreme we can expect Him to have forms and to be of a certain nature beyond our human comprehension.

That isn't just hiding behind an argument; I believe this with all my heart. I believe that God is three in one, and I believe that Christ is one of the three. Jesus Christ is in reality God Himself! This is basically what is being taught here, the reality of His deity.

The second thing that I want you to notice is the equality of Christ's deity. Paul says in verse 6 that He, "being in the form of God, thought it not robbery to be equal with God." Another way to say it is, "He didn't feel that He ought to hang on to His equality with God."

Paul says here, quite categorically, that Jesus Christ was equal with God. And here again people have a hard time accepting this truth. There is only one basis upon which you will ever come to the point of accepting the deity of Christ and the equality of Christ, and that is to accept by faith what the Word of God teaches. The Bible is quite categorical and absolutely dogmatic in this, that the deity of Christ is real and the deity of Christ is equal with the deity of the Father.

But the third thing to notice about *the being* of the Lord Jesus Christ is the humility of His deity. For Paul then goes on to say this—not only did He not feel that He ought to hold on to His position of equality but that He "made himself of no reputation" (v. 7), or a better translation, "He emptied Himself." And the great statement about the Lord Jesus Christ is simply this: He really was deity, and His deity was equal with that of the Father; but He did not hang on to that equality. He was prepared to lay aside His position of being in the form of God, to divest Himself of all the trappings of glory, to be made in human likeness and to step from deity into humanity.

Here again, we delve into mysteries. We're talking in terms of Christ being God and Christ being a man. We're talking in terms of deity stepping into humanity, of heaven emptying itself of its greatest treasure and investing itself in earth. Christ accepted the privilege and the responsibility of humbling Himself and coming down to this earth.

If we can put it in human terms, which are quite inadequate, somewhere back in eternity before the worlds were ever made, God the Father and God the Son and God the Holy Spirit had a committee meeting. All three members were there. And they discussed what was going to happen. They had the opportunity of looking into the future before the future ever happened. They knew what was going to happen and they devised what we call, quite inadequately, the plan of salvation. This plan required that God should accept the punishment for sin Himself and thereby demonstrate His love. And as the committee meeting held session it was decided that the Lord Jesus Christ should be the one who should lay aside His glory and all the trappings of His deity to be born as a baby and live as a man and die as a criminal.

If we can talk in these terms, what it really means is this—Jesus Christ voluntarily, in the greatest act of humility that the world has ever known, decided not to hold on to that equal position that was His by right. Willingly and joyfully He emptied Himself of all the trappings of deity and was made in human likeness.

This is a statement that we either accept or reject, but you know what I've discovered? I've found if I accept this it gets right to me, because I am confronted once again with the fact that the Lord Jesus Christ, who was rich, for my sake became poor, in order that I, through His poverty, might be made rich. Christ is supreme in being.

Christ Is Supreme in Life

Now what I want you to notice is this—that Christ is supreme in life. We saw that He emptied Himself and took upon Him the form of a servant. The word *servant* is better translated *slave*. So the passage should read, He "took upon him the form of a slave, and was made in the likeness of men: and being found in fashion as a man, he humbled himself, and became obedient" to God even to the point of death on a cross. Now here we see the sheer supremacy of Jesus Christ in life. We have a revelation of who Christ is in being, which we cannot fully understand; but now we go a step further and see how utterly supreme Christ was in life down here on earth as a man. There are three things I would like to suggest to you:

First, He accepted the servant's place;
Second, He entered a sinful world; and
Third, He adopted a selfless position.

This is beautifully portrayed for us in John, chapter 13. The disciples were all gathered together for a meal. It was customary in those days in the hot, dusty, dry climate, for someone to wash people's feet as they came in. This was an act of the slave, an act of servitude. But it was a necessary service.

Evidently there wasn't a servant present at this gathering. The obvious thing was for one of the followers to decide, "Well, okay, let me do it. I'll do it for you other guys." But unfortunately none of them was prepared to do that. And so I would guess they all sat and looked at each other and waited to see who would make the first move. Who would take his robe off and gird himself with a towel, who would go to get that vase to fill it with water, who would kneel down in front of his friends and pick up their feet and wash them?

And they all looked at each other, and one fellow said to himself, "Well, you needn't think I'm going to do it. I wouldn't wash his feet." And another one looks across and thinks, "Yeah, if he hadn't said what he did say about me I might have done it, but I'm not doing his."

And as all these things were going on in their minds, to their utter amazement the Lord Jesus Christ got up from dinner, took off His robe, got hold of a towel and girded Himself with the towel. He filled a basin full of water and knelt at the first disciple, who happened to be Simon Peter, and took hold of his foot. Simon Peter said, "What do you think you're doing?"

Jesus said, "I'm going to wash your feet, Simon Peter."

Peter said, "You're not going to wash me."

And Jesus said, "If I don't wash you, you have no part in me."

So Peter said, "Okay, wash all of me!"

Jesus said, "I don't need to wash all of you; you have been cleansed, you just need to have your feet washed."

Here you have the remarkable illustration of the Lord Jesus Christ in His humility. When He took off His outer robe, He was demonstrating the fact that He laid aside the trappings of deity. When He girded Himself with the towel, He was illustrating the fact that He accepted the servant's place. When He knelt in front of His inferiors, He was demonstrating how He could handle Himself. When He picked up their feet and washed them, He was showing how far a man can stoop in his demonstration of love.

Here's the funny thing—everybody says that Jesus Christ was the greatest man who ever lived, or at least one of the greatest who ever lived. But for some strange reason we all deny the principles that made Him great. He never did any of the things *we* say you have to do if you're going to be great. In fact, He flatly contradicted the things that we insist that you've got to do if you're going to be great. The Lord Jesus summarized it very beautifully. "He that is going to be greatest among you has got to learn to be a servant." (See Matt. 23:11.)

Why is it that people say Jesus Christ was a great man if they deny and reject all the principles of His existence, of His humility, of His self-effacements, of His abandonment, and of His desire to serve—the willingness to bow the knee and the willingness to wash His servants' feet? Why is it that we think He is so great? Why aren't we prepared to have the same mind and the same attitude?

You know the world is in a mess, but do you know *why* it is in a mess? The world is in a mess because everybody's sticking up for his own rights. And everybody insists on being his own person, and everybody wants to do his own thing. And everybody does what's right in his own eyes, and everybody insists on being number one, and everybody wants everybody else to accept him as number one. We've got a world populated by millions upon millions of people all doing "their own thing." Everyone does that which is right in his own eyes, and nobody is prepared to take the first step to humble himself and make himself available to others instead of expecting others to be available to him.

And yet the answer is very simple—"Let the mind of Christ be in you." Because if Jesus Christ was so great as a man, why don't we try being great—His way! Then we would accept the servant's place instead of wanting to be the boss. And we would be prepared to enter into a sinful world instead of trying to keep away from it all. We would adopt a selfless position instead of just being interested in "our own thing," and just filling our lives with number one. Jesus Christ was totally supreme in being and utterly supreme in life.

You know, I'm always interested in the people who insist that Jesus Christ was the greatest man who ever lived but deny that He was God, because they've got themselves argued into an awful corner. They have to answer an awful problem: Why would a man say he was God if he wasn't?

I think that there are only two reasons: he was crazy, or he was a rogue. So the man who says that Jesus was the greatest man who ever lived, but wasn't the God that He claimed to be, is in the position of saying that the greatest man who ever lived was a rogue, or the greatest man who ever lived was crazy, or the greatest man who ever lived was a crazy rogue.

Some people say, "Jesus was just a great teacher." But the funny thing about His teaching was this—He finished up with only twelve pupils. It hardly seems that He was the greatest teacher who ever lived if He finished up with only twelve pupils. His message or His teaching just didn't click. He finished up with twelve students, none of whom got the message and every one of whom flunked. He taught a very simple message: "I'm going to die and rise again." Only twelve people stuck with Him, and not one of them believed that He would rise again from the dead!

His disciples made no preparations for His resurrection; the only people who did make preparations for it were His enemies, who had a sneaking suspicion something funny was going to happen.

They say He was the greatest man who ever lived, but He was not God. If so, He was a rogue and a liar and crazy. They say He was the greatest teacher who ever lived, yet He finished up with twelve students, all of whom flunked.

You must either accept what Jesus said about Himself and agree that He was the greatest man who ever lived; that He was God who humbled Himself and became a man. Or you must say, "Forget the whole business! He was a phony."

When I acknowledge that Jesus Christ was real and that He was supreme in life, I've got to ask myself, "What made Him big?" And the answer comes out loud and clear: He humbled Himself. That's how a great man becomes great. Christ is supreme in death.

He humbled Himself in life, and He humbled Himself in death. Verse 8 says this: "Being found in fashion as a man, he humbled himself, and became obedient unto death, even the death of the cross." That doesn't mean that He obeyed death, but that He obeyed His Father to the point of death.

People say many things about the death of the Lord Jesus. Some will say, "Well, He was a revolutionary and all revolutionaries get what's coming to them in the end." Others say, "No, it was more than that. He was a brave man and the purpose of His death was to show how brave men should die."

Others say, "He was an idealist who lived a few centuries ahead of his time. The people weren't ready for His idealism and they were convicted by it, so they put Him away. He was just an idealist who came to an unfortunate, sticky end."

Others say, "No, He was a mystic. People who are realists don't like mystics, and so they have to get a mystic out of the system."

All these theories of the death of the Lord Jesus Christ

are diametrically opposed to the truth that is revealed to us in the Word of God, that His death was simply the outcome of His obedience to His Father. The death of the Lord Jesus wasn't a glorious plan coming unstuck, and it wasn't a great man dying for his ideals, and it wasn't a revolutionary coming to a sticky end. The death of the Lord Jesus Christ was God humbling Himself to the Father's will and making Himself obedient to the point of death.

Why on earth would God want His Son to become man and to die on the cross? I would suggest three things to you. First of all, it was an integral part of the divine plan. The plan was not merely for Jesus to come into the world. If He had just come into the world He would have showed us God and burned us up by the revelation. If Jesus had come into the world to show us what man is supposed to be like, all He would have done was drive us into the ground with conviction.

But an integral part of the plan of God was that Jesus Christ should come into the world and that He should live and die—for His life would condemn us, but His death would save us.

Second, His death was an indispensable factor of the divine plan. God's plan is to restore men and women to Himself, and an indispensable factor in the restoration of fallen mankind to a holy God is the death of Christ. It is only on the basis of the death of Christ that mankind can ever be reconciled to God.

God loves people, but He hates their sin. He must demonstrate His love for people and He must demonstrate His hatred for sin at one and the same time. The only way He could do it was in the cross. In the cross of the Lord Jesus Christ we see the greatest demonstration of love that the world has ever known, and we see the greatest demonstration of hatred that the world has ever known. Any time I want to know how much God loves sinners, I look at the cross, and any time I want to see how much

God hates sin, I look at the cross. I see them both there.

And I see Christ being "obedient unto death, even the death of the cross," in order that my sin might be dead in Him and God might be in a position to forgive me. So the cross of Christ was totally supreme. Christ was even supreme at the moment of death when He dismissed His Spirit and cried with a loud voice, "Finished," and accomplished the work that the Father had given Him to do.

Third, His death is an indisputable evidence of His divine love, which we've already talked about.

The Lord Jesus Christ is supreme whichever way you look at it. Supreme in being, the reality of His deity, the equality of His deity, the humility of His deity. Supreme in life, He accepted a servant's place, He entered a sinful world, He adopted a selfless position. He's supreme in death, for His death was an integral part of the divine plan, an indispensable factor and an indisputable evidence of divine love.

Christ Is Supreme in Glory

But I'm glad the story doesn't end there. So often we get the impression that that is the message of the gospel. But then we read that "God also hath highly exalted him" (v. 9). So we see Christ supreme in glory. The great message of the gospel is that Jesus stepped from the heights down to the depths, to the death of the cross which was the criminal's excruciatingly agonizing death. Christ died on the cross and went down into the realm of departed spirits.

But the Bible teaches us that God had no intention of leaving Him there. And so God highly exalted Him. That speaks to me of three things. First, it speaks of Resurrection. The greatest bedrock of the Christian faith is the resurrection of Jesus Christ from among the dead. If Jesus Christ is not risen, our faith is vain. I'll go back to banking and you can go play golf on Sunday mornings if Jesus

Christ is not risen from the dead.

But if Jesus Christ *is* risen from the dead, this is the greatest truth this world has ever known. When God raised Christ from the dead He defeated all that ever defeated a human being. The resurrection of Jesus Christ turned the greatest tragedy to the greatest triumph the world has ever known. Jesus Christ rose again from the dead and God exalted Him.

I remember an old preacher saying a long time ago, "When God looked down from heaven and saw what man had done to His Son, He said, 'You have done your worst. Now I'm going to do My best.'" When man had done his worst to God's Son and crucified Him, God did His best and raised Him from the dead. And then God highly exalted Him.

But the Resurrection was just the beginning of this great exaltation. For we read that He gave Him "a name which is above every name" (v. 9). If the Resurrection is a picture of someone going from tragedy to triumph, the Ascension is the picture of someone going from earth to heaven, and people don't do that too often.

I don't know any human being who was able to lift himself up by his own boot straps and end up in heaven. I have fun with young people sometimes, I give them a bucket and say, "Hey stand in that bucket." So they stand in the bucket and I say, "I'll give you a quarter if you can lift yourself up off the ground." And they think it's the easiest quarter they ever earned. And so they get hold of the thing and they start pulling and tugging and nothing happens.

And so I say, "Will you give me a quarter if I can do it?" And they say, "Sure," and so I simply reach over and pick the bucket up with them in it. And they say, "Oh, I didn't mean that." While no one can lift himself up by his own boot straps or exalt himself in his own bucket, the power outside him can. The glorious picture of the exaltation of

Christ is this, that God raised Him from the dead, therefore giving us the Saviour of victory.

But then God raised Him to His own right hand into heavenly places, giving us our hope for eternity. What hope is there for men and women to enter into heaven if someone hasn't blazed the trail before him? God exalted His Son, and not only gave us a taste of victory and resurrection, but also gave us a taste of eternity through His ascension.

The third thing about His exaltation is His coronation. The literal translation is *"The Name*—which is above every name."* When it talks about names it speaks about authority. God took Christ from the depths and raised Him to the heights. He put everything under His feet and gave Him the name, King, Lord of lords, Law of all law givers. And God looks down from heaven and says, "I care not what you think of My Son. This is what *I* think about My Son." He exalted Him by resurrection, and He exalted Him by ascension and by coronation. He has *the name.*

Fourth, Christ is supreme in glory. I need to be constantly reminded that Jesus Christ who has come to live within me isn't just an influence. He isn't just a power. I need to be constantly reminded of the total supremacy of the Lord Jesus because He is the One who is exalted at the Father's right hand, with all things put under His feet. I need to have my sense of holy awe and holy reverence constantly stimulated. He is utterly supreme, supreme in being, in life, and death, and glory.

Christ Is Supreme in Eternity

Fifth, Christ is supreme in eternity. We read in verses 10 and 11, "That at the name of Jesus every knee should bow, of things in heaven, and things in earth, and things under the earth; and that every tongue should confess that Jesus Christ is Lord, to the glory of God the Father."

People often say to me, "What on earth is the world

coming to?" If you ever hear anybody say that you know what to tell them. Just say, "Every knee will bow, in heaven and earth and under the earth, and every tongue will confess that Jesus Christ is Lord," and they'll look at you as if you're nuts. People will wriggle and argue and will try to evade it and avoid it. The funny thing about it is they can wriggle and evade and avoid it all they want, but they cannot refute it. Because no one, at the very least, knows any better.

But if I accept the statement of Scripture, the world is coming to the point of total subjection to Christ, so that every knee will bow to Him. And the world is coming to total acknowledgement of Christ, so that every tongue will confess Him. And the world is coming to absolute vindication of Christ. Jesus Christ is Lord.

I live my life in the light of this truth. If there will be a day that I have to acknowledge Christ as Lord, I want to start practicing now. And if there's going to be a day when every tongue will confess Jesus Christ as Lord, I want to practice now. And I don't want to get away with as little as possible down here on earth; I want to be, now, what I'm going to be then. I want to start training for what I'm going to be then.

If Jesus Christ was Lord and is Lord and will be Lord, and everybody's going to admit it, He will settle for nothing less than being the Lord He is now. It means my knee subjected to Him now, it means my tongue confessing Him now, it means my life vindicating Him now.

We need once again a taste and a reminder of the sheer supremacy of Jesus Christ who is Lord.

Christ Supreme in Christians

This brings us to the sixth point—Christ supreme in Christians. Paul says, "Let this mind be in you." How on earth are Christians going to be different from everybody else? How on earth is the church going to be different from any other establishment? How on earth can the fellowship of believers show the world which way to go? There's only one way; to have in the individual Christian the mind of Christ. And this is a command. See to it, every Christian, that the mind of Christ is in you.

What's the mind of Christ? The mind of Christ is this, that if I humble myself, God will exalt me. If I'll go to the death of a cross, resurrection will be inevitable. If I'm risen I will live on a higher plane and people will begin to see that Christ is Lord.

"Let this mind be in you." The hardest thing for a Christian to do is to accept to himself the mind and attitude of Christ, and to reject his own selfish life. The hardest thing for a Christian is to acknowledge that the way to a resurrection life is through the cross. The hardest thing for a Christian is to admit that the only way for the dynamic of God to be released is to humble himself. And the hardest thing for a Christian to admit is that the only way to exaltation is through self-abasement.

But the Lord Jesus taught it. He said, "Except a corn of wheat fall into the ground and die, it abideth alone; but if it die, it bringeth forth much fruit" (John 12:24). And I believe that the degree to which I know the crucifixion of Christ and death to myself, is the degree to which the resurrection life of Jesus Christ will be released in me and through me. "Let this mind be in you."

Christ Supreme in Your Town
The final point is this—that Christ was intended to be supreme in Philippi, which seems a far cry from being supreme in glory. But we don't just live in the light that He will be supreme in glory in eternity. He wants to be supreme in your town. And how is Christ going to be supreme in your town and in Philippi? The literal translation in the beginning of verse 5 is, "Let this mind be among you (plural)." We're not just to have this attitude individu-

ally, but we're to have this attitude collectively among ourselves. When this attitude is seen among a group of people it is so unique it is unbelievable. People will begin to watch and say, "Hey, what's going on there? These people seem to want to serve each other, they seem to want to humble themselves before each other, they seem to want to bow their knee to God, they seem to want to be resurrected among each other by the power of God. What's going on among these people? They're not just selfish people, they're not just living for themselves, going their own way. They're not governed by the things that govern everybody else, and they're not laying up treasures for themselves as everybody else. What's going on in their lives?"

I'd say a cross and a Resurrection have gone into their lives. The mind of Christ is operating in them and among them. And when the mind of Christ is operative among a group of people, do you know what it means? It means a totally different attitude not only to the Lord but to each other.

"Let this mind be in you, which was also in Christ Jesus." A mind shattered by the supreme sacrifice of Christ, a mind excited by the supreme exaltation of Christ and a life abandoned to a living Christ.

When I was a child I heard Dr. Donald Grey Barnhouse speak at the Keswick Convention in England. He surveyed the audience and then he said, "The way to up is down." And there was a kind of rustle among the British crowd—that's hardly the way to begin a sermon. He waited till the slight rustle ended and then he said, "The way to down is up." And I looked at him from my hard seat in the back row and said to myself, "That American preacher is a nut." And I switched him off and I'm sorry. Because, if as a kid I could have learned that, I might have saved myself and others a lot of trouble.

What he, Dr. Barnhouse, was saying was this—If you want to go up, the way to do it is to go down. But if you insist on pushing yourself up, God will accept full responsibility for pushing you right down. That is diametrically opposed to all human principles, but it's the way God works. We have the loveliest of all illustrations in Christ. The way to the throne was through the tomb. The way to the crown is through the cross. The way to Christ's exaltation, and the exaltation of millions of redeemed souls, was through the agony of Calvary. The way to a life lived in the power of God down here on earth is through humility and bowing the knee to Christ as Lord. It starts when I as a sinner come to the foot of the cross and say, "Lord Jesus, forgive me. Lord Jesus, change me, and by the power of your resurrection life, lift me up. Set me on a higher plane." The way to up is down. But if you don't want that, if you're going to be going the wrong way, be absolutely sure of this—the way to down is up. "But let this mind be in you which was also in Christ Jesus."

Questions for Discussion

1. What is your understanding of the Trinity? How would you explain it to a skeptical college student? How would you explain it to a questioning child?

2. When was the last time you laid aside the privileges of rank and position in order to better serve the Lord?

3. Have you washed any feet—done any "dirty" jobs— for your fellow believers lately?

4. In what areas of your life is Christ's supremacy most evident? Which areas need to be brought under submission?

6

WHO DOES WHAT?

Wherefore, my beloved, as ye have always obeyed, not as in my presence only, but now much more in my absence, work out your own salvation with fear and trembling. For it is God which worketh in you both to will and to do of his good pleasure. Do all things without murmurings and disputings: that ye may be blameless and harmless, the sons of God, without rebuke, in the midst of a crooked and perverse nation, among whom ye shine as lights in the world; holding forth the word of life; that I may rejoice in the day of Christ, that I have not run in vain, neither labored in vain.

Philippians 2:12-16

Some words are harder to take than others. For instance, *love, joy* and *peace* aren't half so hard to live with as *obedience, responsibility* and *discipline*. But all of them have their place in the Christian vocabulary.

The Command to Obey

"Wherefore, my beloved, as ye have always obeyed . . . . " (v. 12). The subject of obedience is introduced by the word "wherefore," which links it to the previous verses which speak of the obedience of Christ even to the death of the cross. The results of His obedience, among other things, where that He is now exalted to the heights of glory where every knee will bow to Him and every tongue confess that He is Lord. But it was obedience that put Him there, and, therefore, the Christian should regard obedience, not as an onerous chore, but as an evidence of Christ's nature within him.

Work Out

We can't talk of obedience without stipulating that to which obedience is required. The command is quite clear, however: "Work out your own salvation" (v. 12). The command is clear, but the understanding of it is far from clear.

The confusion arises from differing answers to the question, "How can people be saved, justified and forgiven, and receive eternal life?" As a reward for their own efforts, or as a gift from the grace of God? The idea that we can earn salvation is very attractive. It appeals to our egos.

Some people say, "I never accept anything that I haven't earned and deserved." This is nonsense, for such a person didn't earn the gift of life itself, does nothing to deserve his life's breath and is incapable of survival outside of the provision of God and the support of society, neither of which he produced. Many people of this persuasion point to verse 12 and say, "There you are, you've got to work it out yourself."

The other view is more humiliating. It insists that mankind, because of sinfulness, cannot merit salvation; but may receive it as a gift from the loving heart of God made possible through the work of Christ on the cross. This is the clear teaching of Scripture, but, "Work out your own salvation," seems to contradict.

There is no real problem with this when we take the whole passage in context. "For it is God which worketh in you" is the next part of the statement. If God is working in a person, then salvation has already taken place as far as initial experience is concerned. Therefore, the verse does not speak of initial salvation in terms of forgiveness of sin and reconciliation to God, but of that ongoing experience of salvation that is the product of a right relationship with God.

In other words, if you have been saved by grace through faith, you'd better be obedient to God and "work out" what God has started within.

First, let us see something of the *responsibility* of this outworking. Always remember that imperatives are to be obeyed, and that obedience is a moral responsibility. God in His great wisdom made human beings morally responsible. It is popular in some areas of Christian thought to downgrade the necessity for human responsibility. This is partly because the Bible sometimes uses expressions that give the impression that mankind is a passive vehicle through which God works. God is the potter, we are the clay; Christ is the vine, we are the branches, and so on . . . . Mankind is certainly the instrument, the vessel that God uses, but we are also the agents who gladly accept the responsibility of cooperating with God. We are branches, and we are clay, but we are also ambassadors, soldiers, servants, watchmen, and children. And all these positions are responsible in the extreme.

What, then, is the responsibility of which Paul speaks? It is the responsibility of being what you are called to be and doing what you are told to do.

The *reality* of this is what we need to look into next. As we have already seen, obedience is crucial. Salvation is going to work out through your pores in the degree in which you are obedient. That is a cold reality. C.T. Studd, the great missionary pioneer, was sharing a room with a colleague on one of their journeys. The young man awoke before daybreak to discover C.T. huddled in the corner of the room, wrapped in a blanket, poring over his well-thumbed Bible in the light of a sputtering candle.

"What are you doing?" he enquired.

C.T. replied, "I couldn't sleep because I felt I had something wrong in my relationship with the Lord, and so I have been reading through the New Testament to check on His commands to me in case I have been disobedient."

It is that kind of desire for obedience that shows a watching world that the salvation of God is working out.

Another reality of this outworking is humility. "Fear and trembling" sounds a little strange to our ears. It means "reverence and healthy respect." It is most unfortunate that some people get the idea that because salvation is free it is cheap. To some the idea of eternal security is a license for ill-disciplined, careless living. "I'm saved whatever I do. What I do is not going to affect my destiny. I'm saved by grace, so if I go wrong I'll just claim grace and go on from there." Perhaps Paul had this in mind when he reminded the people that a sense of humble gratitude and reverential awe is more befitting a saved soul than careless and disobedient living.

It is great to know that the Lord Jesus called us friends, but if we treat Him as casually as we treat our friends, and lose all sense of His majesty and power, we miss much of the serious humble life that is evidence of our salvation. It is wonderful to be part of a vibrant Christian fellowship that is relaxed and happy, but it is disastrous to be part of a Christian experience that lacks solemnity in the presence of God and commitment in the service of God.

Paul also gives two insights into his own ministry of "working it out." He talks of running and laboring in verse 16. These are expressions which will recur in the epistle, so we will pause only to say that our salvation will show itself in the sense of urgency that we exhibit, like a runner in a race, and the sense of commitment in the cause of Christ that we demonstrate by laboring in His service. There is no such urgency and involvement in many believers' lives, and in this they are being disobedient. The command is "work it out."

Shine It Out
"Do all things without murmurings and disputings: that ye may be blameless and harmless, the sons of God, without rebuke in the midst of a crooked and perverse nation, among whom ye shine as lights in the world" (vv. 14,15). The word *lights* means *luminaries;* that is, the moon and sun and the stars. Please notice Paul's way to be a star! See how you can be the sun to give light by day and the moon to give light by night! That is your responsibility.

Blameless is the first word used. This kind of blamelessness means that we should deal with the things in our lives that stick out like sore thumbs. There is no way that a professional grumbler can shine. The grumbling has to go if the shining is to start. Argumentative people who specialize in friction and division are no credit to the message of Christ and His salvation. Moses' face shone, and he didn't know it; but if you are constantly grumbling or arguing or whining or troublemaking, you won't be shining and everyone will know it!

Harmless sounds a bit anemic. But in the original language it has the connotation of something that is pure, sincere, without any added commodities. In other words, "for real." He is a real child of God who believes like one and behaves like one and has nothing in his life that people can get after him about. That's the kind of person that Paul has in mind, and that is the kind of person who does some shining.

Paul's remarks are, on the one hand, encouraging; and on the other, just the opposite. He says we live in a nation (generation) that is twisted and warped and generally fouled up. That is discouraging. But, on the other hand, the darker the scene the less difficult it is to shine. That is encouraging. It is not so difficult as it may appear to shine in today's world, because today's world is so wrong on so many counts that you can shine just by being right. But it requires real honest-to-God living in the light of His Word, and the power of His Spirit.

Hold It Out

"Holding forth the word of life" (v. 16). The *word of life* is a beautiful expression used here to describe God's authoritative statement about life. God has spoken, and when He speaks His Word is of such power that He can even create something out of nothing and raise the dead to life. The Word of life is God's message of good news that Jesus Christ has died and risen so that a dying world might live. This life is power. It is powerful enough to conquer the grave and mighty enough to make the coward brave. It is a Word of life with purpose and content. It is the great good news of the provision of God for the bored and the broken, the dejected and the defeated. It's Life with a capital "L."

But notice what Paul says about it. He insists that we in our daily lives "hold it forth." The Greek word translated here can mean "hold it fast" or "hold it forth." Let's assume that he had both in mind because they are closely related. No one can effectively hold it forth if he does not hold it fast, and anyone holding it fast will know he has to hold it forth.

To hold fast the Word of God is not easy for people living in a secular society. Contemporary society is so estranged from biblical principles that in many instances it doesn't even know what they are. Whether Christians like it or not, they cannot avoid being affected by the philosophies of the surrounding society which constantly bombards them through the media. They live and work with people whose outlook and life-style are foreign to God's requirements. This has an erosive quality, and it takes a very determined Christian to reject the pervasiveness of the opposing society and breathe the fresh air of the Word of life. It takes an awful lot of holding onto. But it must be done!

Then there is the necessity for the believer to hold forth what he is holding fast. To put it bluntly, Christianity involves evangelism. All believers will agree to that, but they may not understand that does not mean leaving it to the professionals. It means all Christians engaging in holding out the Word of life. There are many ways of doing this. You don't have to stand on a street corner holding out a tract, or chant and dance at the nearest airport like a bald-headed devotee of Hare Krishna. But there's nothing to stop your doing that if you feel it is God's way for you to hold out the Word!

Think of your neighborhood and think of ways in which you can acquaint the people there with the "Word of life." Then ask God to propel you into action. Look for the opportunities to hold out the Word, and take them, and if they don't appear, make them. Share what you know and tell what you've discovered. Write letters, give away books, lend tapes, visit friends, relate experiences. Hold it out!

Being saved certainly starts something. What a shock for those who only wanted to escape hell to discover that they have a crushing, frightening, exciting, challenging responsibility. God wants them to work it out and to shine it out and to hold it out. What a jolt for the complacent pew warmer to find out that it is necessary for him to be obedient to the Word he believes and to do what he knows.

The Power to Obey

But wait a minute. All this is so overwhelming that many a believer has sunk without a trace at this point. Others have bravely met the challenge and soldiered on against fearful odds until they could take it no more. Thank the Lord that we have the other half of the coin to consider now.

Remember the golden rule of spiritual experience. When God gives a command He also gives the power to obey. This does not belittle the command or lessen the responsibility. On the contrary, it shows that God takes His own Word so seriously that He makes the power available for it to be obeyed. And it intensifies the responsibility because no one can evade the command of God with any kind of excuse if God's answer to the excuse is, "I gave you the command and I gave you the power; there is nothing else to say."

The Entrance of God

"For it is God which worketh in you both to will and to do of his good pleasure" (v. 13).

There are many ways in which we can look at the relationship of God to mankind. God is overshadowing us, He is going before us, He is close beside us. He is our rear guard, but He is also within us.

God is in us. This is not another of those woolly euphemistic ideas that we're all tired of hearing. You know the thing. "Now we all have a little divine spark in us, and we must all try to fan it." This is not what the Scriptures teach. They say that until we receive Christ we are dead to God, and only when we are regenerated through the operation of the Holy Spirit does God take up His residence within our bodies. But when He does, He really does!

When Christ's presence graced a stable under an inn in Bethlehem, the inn took on new significance. When He enters any place, He makes it strangely different.

When God in Christ entered your life at the moment of your commitment to Him, you took on new significance. You were no longer little old you against the big cold world. You became little old you, the residence of the *mighty, eternal God.* Little old you and the mighty, eternal God sharing one body, one life, one world and one society. What do you think could happen to your life and your world as a result?

It all depends on what God wants to do in you. Paul says He is "working in you." *Energizing* is an English equivalent to the Greek word used here. I like to think of an energetic God living in me. It is good for my inbred laziness. The fact that He is a pulsating God within me is good for my lethargy, and His majestic presence is a constant challenge to my own mediocrity.

The Enjoyment of God

Wonderful as this is, there is more for us to understand. This indwelling energy is within us not for our personal satisfaction or for our theological titillation. He is within us for "His good pleasure." That may sound disappointing to some. They thought He lived in them to make them feel good. That is not His primary purpose. He has some big plans for you, and He is there to implement them. If you bring yourself to want what He wants, then you will find He will work out in your life what you want. Not because *you* want it, but because *He* wants it and you came into line with His desires.

The Energy of God

Do you know how God works out His plan in your life? By energizing your will and mobilizing your doing. Have you ever found yourself wanting to do things that you previously refused to do? Have you ever refused to do something and then gone back and said, "Give me another chance, and I'll do it"? It was God energizing your desiring mechanism and your deciding mechanism so that you desired new desire and were willing to follow His will.

It is God's pleasure that you work out your salvation. He wants you to shine out in a dark world. He requires you to hold out the Word of life. As He lives within you (assuming that you are a redeemed sinner), He will be making these desires and plans very clear to you. Only one thing is necessary for them to leap from the realm of the theologically possible into the light of the practically experiential. And that one thing is obedience.

Jesus was obedient and, as a result, heaven will be full of people bowing at His feet and confessing Him as Lord. Obedience to God's good pleasure did that. Who knows (apart from God) what your obedience will accomplish?

Questions for Discussion

1. How can you reconcile Paul's exhortation to "work out your own salvation" with verses like Ephesians 2:8,9 and Romans 4:2-8?

2. In what ways do you "hold forth the Word of life" in your daily activities? How are you shrinking back from this duty? How can you be more effective?

3. What has God commanded you to do? Has He given you the power to obey? Are you being obedient? If not, what's holding you back?

4. God is willing to "energize" you to do His will. Are you willing to receive His energy?

7

THERE'S JOY IN SERVING JESUS

Yea, and if I be offered upon the sacrifice and service of your faith, I joy, and rejoice with you all. For the same cause also do ye joy, and rejoice with me. But I trust in the Lord Jesus to send Timotheus shortly unto you, that I also may be of good comfort, when I know your state. For I have no man like-minded, who will naturally care for your state. For all seek their own, not the things which are Jesus Christ's. But ye know the proof of him, that, as a son with the father, he hath served with me in the gospel. Him therefore I hope to send presently, so soon as I shall see how it will go with me. But I trust in the Lord that I also myself shall come shortly. Yet I supposed it necessary to send to you Epaphroditus, my brother, and companion in labour, and fellow soldier, but your messenger, and he that ministered to my wants. For he longed after you all, and was full of heaviness, because that ye had heard that he had been sick. For indeed he was sick nigh unto death: but God had mercy on him; and not on him only, but on me also, lest I should have sorrow upon sorrow. I sent him therefore the more carefully that, when ye see him again, ye may rejoice, and that I may be the less sorrowful. Receive him therefore in the Lord with all gladness; and hold such in reputation: because for the work of Christ he was nigh unto death, not regarding his life, to supply your lack of service toward me.

Philippians 2:17-30

Joy was never far from the thoughts and experience of Paul as he wrote this letter. It was not because his circumstances were conducive to joy, but because his relationship to Christ was bringing him joy. This is even more remarkable when we read, "Yea, and if I be offered upon the sacrifice and service of your faith, I joy, and rejoice with you all" (v. 17). He was referring, of course, to the very real possibility of his own execution. But even this he regarded as a spiritual exercise and anticipated it with joy.

The expression *offered* is a striking one straight from the Old Testament. The priests, when they offered sacrifices to God on behalf of the people, would sometimes pour wine on the sacrifice. This was called a libation. When Paul thinks of the possibility of his blood being poured out in martyrdom, he sees it as a libation on the sacrifice of the Philippian believers' faith. In other words, he is presenting the believing Philippians as his offering to God, and his own poured-out life is an added libation. And all this is designed to bring delight to the Lord he serves. Let's look at Paul's view of Christian service in this light, for it holds many insights we need today.

The Delights of Christian Service

Oswald Smith captured something of this in his hymn, "Joy in Serving Jesus." Unfortunately, this is not everyone's experience. Far too many do not wish to serve Him, and many others serve Him with something less than joy. Perhaps it is because real service requires the servant to be personally poured out to God as a sacrifice, a libation. This runs contrary to our own selfishness, but it is the basis of delight in serving Christ. If service is done with any degree of reticence or halfheartedness, it will be a chore instead of a joy.

There is absolutely no substitute for the "living sacrifice" that God asks of us in Romans 12:1, but we often struggle against it and are miserable as a result. The joy

comes when we hold back no longer and pour ourselves
out to God, ready and willing for His least demand. Perhaps this kind of pouring out is best described by the
words of commitment often used in meetings in England.
"I am willing to serve you anywhere, at any time, under
any circumstances." That says it all.

But then there is pouring out of yourself into other
people. Paul gives ample evidence of having done this.
Timothy is one of the products of his ministry in Lystra.
Here was a young man, seemingly shy, reserved, suffering
from stomach problems, but a stalwart of the faith.
Epaphroditus was another: a product of Paul's ministry in
Philippi who had almost died as a result of his enthusiastic
involvement in the work of the Lord.

Paul had poured himself into these men, and they were
pouring themselves into others. Epaphroditus was doing
so much pouring that he was "not regarding his own life"
(v. 30). The word Paul uses is a gambling word which
really means he was prepared to gamble, to take risks with
his own well-being, for the sake of the ministry. When you
get to that stage of commitment it becomes a joy to serve
Jesus.

The Design of Christian Service

Any activity must have an objective; without one nothing of lasting significance results. What is the objective of
Christian service? The overriding objective is that God
should be glorified, but this is such an abstract idea that we
tend to forget that it can be achieved only in concrete
terms. What, then, should be the objective of our
service—what concrete happenings will glorify God?

Paul regards the faith that the Philippians had exer-
cised as an offering that he is presenting to God for His
satisfaction. He has labored to introduce these people to
the concept of faith, to bring them to an experience of
faith, and to encourage them to grow in faith. I believe that

this is a concrete objective of all ministry.

It is not easy to introduce people to the concept of faith as a principle of divine acceptance. People have been conditioned to believe that mankind is the master of its own destiny and the solver of its own problems. Modern society is riddled with a humanistic philosophy that preaches the wonderful omnipotence and omniscience of mankind. This gospel has been preached so well and believed so deeply that most people are convinced that the answer to mankind's problems lies in mankind's ability to solve them.

Even man's spiritual problems can be solved by his own careful attention to doing what he thinks he ought and not doing what he thinks he shouldn't. He thinks that God will ultimately reward him with the blessings he needs. There is nothing of faith in this except man's implicit faith in his own ability to do what God says he is unable to do.

Introduce someone to the concept of dependence upon God for salvation instead of dependence on self, and you have done a great work of ministry that will bring delight to God. What pleases God more than to have people come to understand that He is not to be ignored but trusted? What can honor Him more than to get this over to the masses who at worst think He is dead and at best consider Him irrelevant?

But it is not enough to introduce people to a principle. We need to take them on into the experience of putting their faith in Christ. Remember the Philippian jailer coming to faith in such a tempestuous fashion, and Lydia coming to trust Christ? This is where the joy of serving comes.

Then when you have the thrill of leading someone to faith in Christ, you have the task of teaching him to live by faith now that he has been saved by faith. This is the essence of Christian service and it takes a lifetime to teach it.

Would you say that your service has design to it? You are not stumbling along reluctantly and aimlessly, but you know what you are doing? God is working in you so effectively that you are making definite inroads into your society and seeking men and women rejecting what Paul calls "a crooked and perverse nation" and taking their stand in Christ? Can you put your finger on your Timothy or Epaphroditus and offer him as a sacrifice to the Lord?

The Dynamic of Christian Service

We have repeatedly touched on the subject of service, but Paul finds it necessary, so presumably we should too. Notice that on two occasions Paul says, "I trust in the Lord" (vv. 19,24). It is interesting that he uses two different Greek words to express his feelings of dependence on and confidence in the Lord. This, as we have already seen, is the dynamic principle that releases the power of God and the purposes of God in our lives.

Dependence is a present tense experience. As you sit in an airplane you depend upon it to hold you up at that moment, but you also (presumably) have confidence in it for your immediate future, that it will deliver you to your destination. So it is with the Lord. We can have present tense dependence on Him for the "now" and complete confidence in Him for the "when."

This was Paul's theology, but it was beautifully expressed in his life-style and that of his fellow workers. Only a person of confidence and dependence could take on the job that Timothy accepted. Stomach trouble included! Epaphroditus' dependence and confidence stuck out all over the place when he gambled with his life for Christ's sake. And Paul, as we have seen repeatedly, lived it constantly in his prison cell.

The Depths of Christian Service

Take note of three little words that are full of importance. One is the word *know*. Paul wants to *know* their state (v. 19). This is indicative of his interest in people.

There is a tendency in our pragmatic, computerized society to overlook the value of the individual. Even in the work of the ministry, statistics can replace people and planning can be substituted for caring. I am painfully aware of the fact that as a work of God grows, personal contact wanes. But I am convinced that there is no substitute for real interest in people, however busy we may be.

Paul never ceases to amaze me—he remembered people so clearly even though he had mixed with the multitudes and preached to the world. He had a concern for the individual that never waned even in the midst of the most trying circumstances.

One day an evangelist of worldwide renown told me of one of the greatest influences on his early life. A well-known man of a previous generation took him aside to discover what this boy really had in his heart. Interest in people is imperative for in-depth service.

Then there is the little word *comfort.* This is something of which Paul often spoke. He had needs that could only be met through others, and he knew that some of the needs of others were going to be met through him. So he says that he wants to know how they are so that he "may be of good comfort" (v. 19). This speaks of his involvement with people.

Many people today would love to disprove John Donne's theory that "no man is an island." They would just love to be able to get along without any sense of involvement in people's lives, and they would appreciate it immensely if people would get out of theirs. But they are missing something vital when they operate this way.

Epaphroditus had learned this from Paul, too. Look at his feelings for the people in Philippi. Paul says, "He longed after you all, and was full of heaviness" (v. 26), which means quite literally he was homesick for the fellowship of the believers in Philippi.

Do you have any people in your church who like to

come in late, sit in the back row, say nothing to anybody, slip out early and disappear into their woodwork for another week before launching out into another exercise of magnificent noninvolvement? They certainly don't know much about the depth of Christian service.

Then I want you to look at the third word, *care*. Paul speaks of a surprising problem that he encountered in the Roman church. It was a going concern, but there was a bad flaw. Paul had repeatedly told the Roman Christians of his concern for the Philippians and had asked for someone to volunteer to go to them. The people had listened to him, agreed with him, proposed the motion that "something should be done," seconded it, passed it unanimously and done nothing about it. He couldn't get anybody to go to Philippi. Why? Because he couldn't find anyone to "care" for their well-being (v. 20).

The reason was not that they didn't care, and it wasn't that they couldn't care enough. They were all very careful about seeking "their own, not the things which are Jesus Christ's" (v. 21). They didn't care enough about the work of the Lord among the Philippian people to regard it as their privilege to make an investment of themselves in other people.

That is what it means *to care*. To care enough that you want to devote time and energy and ability in the lives of others for the glory of God. This type of depth is missing in much of our Christian service. The person who cares for his own things to the exclusion of the things of God and the needs of people has missed the boat of Christian service. Take time out today to check on your interest, your involvement and your investment in the people around you. Because these things are a measure of the depth of your service.

The Discipline of Christian Service

I suppose Paul was a little biased about Timothy and

Epaphroditus, but who wouldn't be? They were great servants of God, and Paul had known them from way back when they had made their initial commitment to Christ.

A few years ago I stood on the banks of a river in South America and watched a young man in western clothes climb out of a primitive canoe. The veteran missionary with whom I was traveling beamed at the young man and whispered to me, "The first time I saw him he was a naked Indian kid standing right on this bank, and he pulled in my canoe for me. God gave me a real concern for him, and eventually he came to Christ, committed himself to the Lord's work and is just returning home after graduating from seminary in Costa Rica." I could understand the beam in the missionary's face, and I think Paul beamed when he talked of his co-workers. And he had good cause to be thrilled with them.

Speaking of Timothy, he says, "Ye know the proof of him . . . " (v. 22). The word *proof* means *caliber.* You know what he's made of because he has shown it over and over again. Then note what he says about Epaphroditus. He calls him "brother . . . companion . . . fellow soldier . . . messenger" (v. 25).

Unreserved Commitment

In these few words we see these two as men of serious outlook and determined discipline. No one could earn the title "fellow" from Paul or be regarded as a "soldier" by him without real discipline of life. It is a strange thing that the community of Christians in today's world who are conscious of the early disciples and regard themselves as the modern-day version appear to see little need for the old-time commitment and even less connection between the words "disciple" and "discipline."

Unselfish Attitude

We have already seen that Paul couldn't get anyone to

go from Rome to Philippi, but Timothy had agreed to go in place of a Roman Christian.

Then we also note that Epaphroditus had accepted the job of "messenger" for the Philippians to bring what Paul bluntly called their "lack of service" to him (v. 30). By this he meant that they had committed themselves to support his ministry but had fallen down on the job. Epaphroditus had gotten things moving again and had brought the gift from Philippi to Rome. The point here is that many people were less than enthusiastic about "putting themselves out" to do things like traveling around the Roman world. They would rather stay at home with their families. But these men had a different attitude. They were unselfish!

There is a word that we must not miss in verse 20. The word is *likeminded,* but it means much more than *being of the same opinion.* It is really *like-souled.* In other words, Timothy had "soul" in his ministry. Our black brothers can make a song that is nothing much sound like something out of this world. They put soul into it. Some people put soul into their service and others don't. Some serve the Lord as if they are doing Him a favor, and others serve Him as if He backed them into it, and they can't get out of it. But praise the Lord, there are those who serve with soul.

Unrestrained Enthusiasm

You remember the story of the return of the children of Israel from captivity and their desire to rebuild under the leadership of Ezra and Nehemiah. All who returned to Jerusalem agreed on the rebuilding, but did you ever notice that the nobles "put not their necks to the work"? Their sort are with us today. Not an ounce of enthusiasm do they have for serving the Lord.

The Discouragements of Christian Service

There is so much to be done. Over two billion people

still need to be reached with the gospel of Christ. The opportunities are boundless and the means are with us. But there are so few who appear to be interested. The Romans had trouble finding somebody interested enough to go to Philippi, and the Philippians had trouble finding someone who would go to Rome. The support that had been promised was not forthcoming, and there was too much apathy.

We think that materialism is our invention, but it isn't. The Romans had a bad case of it. "All seek their own" is a pretty stiff comment to make about the situation, but Paul made it. There was so little sacrifice.

This is one of the greatest discouragements that I know. All leaders have to face it. If they are leaders they are people of vision. But there is a good chance that they have not sold their vision to everybody around them. Leaders usually know something of sacrifice, but that doesn't mean that the people they lead have caught the attitude. Therefore, the very nature of leadership presupposes that there will be considerable discouragement for those who take the lead and long to see God at work in the church.

If you get discouraged because you can't get people to see what you see and do what you do and go as fast as you go, remember what Jesus did. He worked with those who meant business. He started with what He had and He began where He was. Discouragement comes when you try to start with what you wish you had but don't have. And it intensifies when you insist on trying to be in a position you are not in, and probably never will be in. So press on, pour out and serve the Lord with gladness!

Questions for Discussion

1. Someone once said that happiness is based upon *happenings* but true joy is based upon certainties. What is your response to this?

2. Are you willing to take risks with your own well-being for the sake of the ministry, as Epaphroditus did?

3. Does the answer to all of mankind's problems lie in its ability to solve them?

4. Who are the people served by your ministry? Are you taking an interest in each individual and his or her place in the Body of Christ?

5. Is your Christian service a disciplined one? What aspects still need to be controlled?

6. When you think of the work to be done to reach the world for Christ, are you discouraged at the enormity of the task or encouraged by the possibilities for God to show His power?

8

REALITY CHRISTIANITY

Finally, my brethren, rejoice in the Lord. To write the same things to you, to me indeed is not grievous, but for you it is safe. Beware of dogs, beware of evil workers, beware of the concision. For we are the circumcision, which worship God in the spirit, and rejoice in Christ Jesus, and have no confidence in the flesh. Though I might also have confidence in the flesh. If any other man thinketh that he hath whereof he might trust in the flesh, I more: Circumcised the eighth day, of the stock of Israel, of the tribe of Benjamin, an Hebrew of the Hebrews; as touching the law, a Pharisee; concerning zeal, persecuting the church; touching the righteousness which is in the law, blameless. But what things were gain to me, those I counted loss for Christ.

Philippians 3:1-7

The words *circumcision* and *concision* aren't on most people's tongues all day long. In fact, *circumcision* sounds a little indelicate and *concision* just isn't in our vocabulary. But for the sake of understanding our next passage of Scripture, they need to be dealt with and understood.

In the Old Testament God made a covenant with Abraham, and the sign and seal of that covenant was circumcision. This act came to have great importance for those who were members of this covenant. It was evidence that they enjoyed a special relationship with God and were part of the people through whom God was planning to bless the world.

Circumcision means literally *to cut around* and, while it referred to a cutting of the foreskin of the male, it was also applied symbolically by the prophets to cutting around people's ears so that they could hear God's Word, and cutting around their lips so they could speak God's message, and cutting around their hearts to get rid of their hardness and rebellion.

The children of Israel became well-known for the circumcision on their physical anatomy, but less well-known for the circumcision of their spiritual lives. They became very technical in their religious observance of circumcision, but lax and indifferent when it came to spiritual realities like open hearts and ears and mouths. It was the old, old story of religion without reality and ritual without response.

The problem was particularly severe in Paul's day because there were a number of men who were all excited about the ritual of circumcision, but less interested in the reality. Paul was just the opposite. He was not concerned in cutting bodies, but he was deeply concerned about circumcised lives. So he draws a distinction between what he calls *the circumcision* (that is, the people who knew spiritual reality as members of God's people, called to fulfill His will) and *the concision* (that is, those people who were hooked on externals and devoid of reality). Incidentally, the word *concision* is of some interest. Ellicott said it was a *studiously contemptuous paranomasia,* which being interpreted is *a rather crude pun!* You could almost say that he was calling them *the butchers!* Be that as it may, the point of this passage is to differentiate between the real and the phony. To show the difference between vital, vibrant Christian reality and cold, correct, rigid religion.

The Reality of Christian Delight

"Rejoice in the Lord" (v. 1) is twice repeated in the fourth chapter, so it has great importance. You will notice that it is an instruction, not a suggestion. Rejoicing in the Lord is not of marginal importance, nor is it an optional extra for evangelical extroverts. It is required because "the joy of the Lord is your strength" (Neh. 8:10).

Strong Christians are strong because they enjoy the Lord. People who don't enjoy Him live their lives unrelated to Him and, accordingly, know nothing of His strength. There is no way a mere human can live in this world as if he belongs to the next world without the strength of the Lord. But if he doesn't enjoy the Lord, he can't enjoy the strength, and he will be a flop to end all flops.

That is why you will often see Christians who make you feel ill just by looking at them. They trip over their bottom lips, and wear faces framed with clouds of gloom. It may well be that they have trouble, even deep trouble. But there is no trouble that merits such attention that it affects a Christian's deportment and demeanor to such an extent. He needs to rejoice in the Lord at the time of trouble and discover strength through Him.

Suppose death hits your family. Deep sorrow and loss will come in its train. But Jesus has conquered death, opened a way into the heavens and promised eternal life to all who trust Him. Now what does that do to a person who in bereavement rejoices in the Lord? It lifts his load and dries his tears and strengthens his resolve. The joy of the Lord is his strength. You can't afford to live other than in enjoyment of the Lord. That is why it is an instruction, not a suggestion.

But you may ask, "How does one rejoice in the Lord?" There are two principles to examine.

Acknowledge His Lordship

To submit to His Lordship is to open yourself up to the plan of God for your life guaranteed by the guiding, controlling hand of the Lord. This produces confidence and joy. However, the Christian who resents the idea of submission and fights the claim of Lordship lives a divided life. And there is no joy in a divided life. Therefore, it is necessary to constantly evaluate your life in the light of Christ's control over different areas of it. Maintain His Lordship day by day.

Accept His Love

You know that the Lord loves you, but do you really enjoy His love? I have often talked to men and women who are having problems with their spouses and asked them about their love for their spouse, and their spouse's love for them. "Do you love your spouse? Does your spouse love you?"

"Yes," they often reply, but there is no spark there. No grin. No delight. They believe, but they don't enjoy it.

I tell them to wake up in the morning and tell their spouses, "I love you," and to stop work for a minute in the middle of the day and think, "Wow, there's someone back home who loves me." I tell them to bask in it, to talk about it, to concentrate on it. In short, to enjoy it.

It is just the same with our enjoyment of the Lord. Think of Him and His love in the morning when you wake up, remember Him in the daytime when you are getting frayed edges on your nerves, rejoice in Him at night as you go to rest. You'll enjoy Him and be stronger as a result.

For example, if you are feeling all the world is against you when it is really only three people in your office, think of the Lord. He's for you, and if He's for you who can be against you? Or if your spouse forgets your anniversary (remember, it's not just *your* anniversary) and you retire to your mirror to pout, convinced that nobody loves you, remember Jesus does. Spend your pouting time praying and praising Him instead. You'll be so strong you'll be teasing your spouse about the omission instead of freezing him or her for the mistake.

The Reality of a Christian's Danger

I like the way Paul insists on warning people of danger in the same breath that he tells them to rejoice. He is conscious that they may think that he is harping on a theme, but he says it is necessary to go on warning them of danger, and so he's going to do it.

The experiences of the Lord's people over the years give us plenty of reasons for repeated warnings. We need to be reminded that there is danger in comfort, for it breeds carelessness. Another reminder always needed is that success breeds smugness. Remember how the children of Israel, flushed with success, rushed to the defeat in one quick, smug stride from Jericho to Ai? Then we need to be told over and over again that satisfaction breeds selfishness. The lepers who discovered the siege of Samaria had been lifted enjoyed their freedom to the hilt, but their fellows died while they feasted. Warnings of danger may not always be appreciated, but they will never become unnecessary.

The Philippians were in danger from "dogs, evil workers, and the concision," and Paul gives a triple "Watch them." The *dogs* were the people who were always looking for a fight, like the ravenous dogs that wandered the streets of Philippi. They're still around. They can soon destroy your joy by getting you in a fight about the choir or the sermon or Billy Graham before you know what's happening. Watch them because your joy in the Lord must not be jeopardized.

The *evil workers* are those who never miss a chance of stirring things up. They major in minors and make issues out of non-issues. They rock the boat and wreck the work wherever they go. Watch them and don't let them!

The *concision,* as we have already seen, are those who discount reality and put ritual at a premium. They butcher people's experience of Christ because of theological niceties and devote their considerable abilities and energies to negative causes. Watch them!

Of course, it could be thought that Paul was getting as negative at this point as those he criticized, but he went on to say, "For we are the circumcision, which worship God in the spirit, and rejoice in Christ Jesus, and have no confidence in the flesh" (v. 3).

The Reality of a Christian's Distinctives
Paul gives us three distinctives of great importance.

The Christian's Distinctive Experience of the Holy Spirit
"We worship God in the spirit." Mankind has an inbuilt desire to worship even when he is so ignorant of truth that he takes a piece of wood left over from his work, carves it into a figure, calls it his god and asks it to deliver him. This is surely the lowest form of worship. However, there are sophisticated forms that are not much higher. They are almost as ludicrous as the form of worship that tells a piece of wood that it made the man who had just carved it! Mod-

ern man worships and adores the products of his own hands and really believes that they are adequate to deliver him. He takes some of the products of his own ingenuity, gives them to the church and puts his implicit faith in these things to deliver him from any demands that God may have upon him.

Then there is the form of worship that is little more than a physical happening—getting the body from bed to pew for an hour a week; sitting when the man says sit, standing when the man says stand, giving when he says give, listening and leaving when he gives the word. Everything that happens is purely physical.

Some people have a higher form of worship. Theirs is aesthetic. They enjoy beautiful surroundings, beautiful music, gorgeous vestments and eloquent speeches. They feel that they should participate, and as they do they feel good. When they leave they feel better for having been there. This is mainly emotional.

There is no denying that worship has its physical, emotional, intellectual and aesthetic aspects, but note again what Paul says, "We worship God in the spirit." The spiritual aspects are those that make worship real. But what is meant by this statement and the parallel saying of the Lord, "They that worship (God) must worship him in spirit and in truth" (John 4:24)?

There is a little ambiguity in some areas of Scripture when the word *spirit* occurs. It may refer to the human spirit or to the Holy Spirit. This is one such area. Paul may be saying, "Worship God in spirit," or, as some scholars believed, "worship by the Spirit of God." Either way there is no insurmountable problem, because to do the first we need the activity of the second. Man worships in his spirit when he worships by the Spirit of God.

This helps to answer the question, "How do we worship?" By depending upon the Spirit of God resident in our spirit "to take the things of Christ and reveal them unto us." This happens through prayerful, careful study of the Word of God. When we open our minds to what the Spirit of God is saying to us through the Word that He inspired, He will begin to make it fit our need and say what needs to be said. This brings us to an understanding of God, and that understanding draws from us a response of praise. This is worship "by the Spirit."

Or God may reveal some great promise in His Word that is relevant to us. The promise demands trust and faith, which we give through the Holy Spirit. This is worship.

Sometimes the Spirit will bring a word of reproof and rebuke, and He will make it convicting to us. Then we must repent and seek reconciliation; when these things are done in the enabling grace of the Spirit that is worship.

Now you will see that this is totally different from the experience of a person sitting in church, dead to the Spirit, going through the motions, but really not worshiping. The Spirit of God, whom he does not know, is not revealing things to him about God, or showing him God's promises, or rebuking him of things for which he should repent. He is engaging in the identical physical actions and is situated in the same aesthetic surroundings as the "true worshiper," but he is not worshiping in the Spirit.

The Christian's Distinctive Exultation in Jesus Christ

We "rejoice in Christ Jesus" (v. 3). This word *rejoice* means *to glory* or *to boast*. Now we all have our little areas of boasting, and we enjoy our moments of glory, even if we are so sanctified that the only thing we ever brag about is our kids or our grandchildren! There are some things that are so meaningful to us that we have to speak with enthusiasm about them. When the Lord is meaningful the distinctive Christian brags on Him.

It's a strange thing, but many Christians feel uneasy talking about the Lord. Sometimes they are afraid of sounding sanctimonious, and I can understand their reticence if that is their problem. At other times they are unsure how they will come across, and that is understandable. But if the reason they don't say anything is that they don't know anything, or what they know does not thrill them, then that is neither understandable nor acceptable.

"Come and hear our preacher, he's the greatest," is not exactly bragging on the Lord. "We've got the fastest growing church east of the Mississippi," isn't bragging on Him either. Now both these facts may be perfectly true, and if they are they may as well be stated. But it would be far better to say, "God is blessing our church so beautifully and we're so glad that He gave us a pastor who preaches the Word of God so that we know what God has to say to us. It is such a thrill. Why don't you come with us sometime?" That puts the glory right where it belongs.

Naturally the "concision" were not bragging on the Lord Jesus. They were more interested in outward forms than in personal relationships with Him. But just look at the difference in Paul. He says, "I count all things but loss for the excellency of the knowledge of Christ Jesus my Lord" (v. 8). We will get into this later, but just note carefully the beautiful personal statement, "Christ Jesus *my* Lord." The Lord Jesus is so precious to Paul in His capacity of Lord that everything else is secondary. That is a sign of a realistic, distinctive Christian experience.

I have often thought how Paul's experience grew and matured even though he had none of the aids to growth that we take for granted. He had no preacher in his cell, no beautiful church building in his prison, no hymnbook to sing from and no fellowship to enjoy. Just Jesus. Maybe that was why he learned to brag on Him, instead of the things that are nothing more than aids to getting to know Him.

The Christian's Distinctive Expression of Self-Distrust

"And have no confidence in the flesh . . . " (v. 3). The word *flesh* is the key to this statement. It was a favorite word of Paul and the other biblical writers, and it has all kinds of meanings. W.E. Vine points out fourteen different meanings in the New Testament alone. So it is no easy matter interpreting it at times.

However, the way to interpret Scripture is to take things in their context and to try to discover the obvious meaning in the light of that context. *Flesh* can be that part of you that hangs between bone and skin. And sometimes this is the meaning in the New Testament, but it cannot be the meaning intended here. What is distinctively Christian about having no confidence in a flabby stomach?

The following verses go on to explain what "confidence in the flesh" meant to Paul. It was having confidence in religious heritage: "circumcised the eighth day, of the stock of Israel, of the tribe of Benjamin, an Hebrew of the Hebrews . . . " (v. 5). It was having great pride in religious knowledge and practice: "as touching the law, a Pharisee . . . " (v. 5). It was being proud of his enthusiastic involvement in a campaign that he felt was valid: "concerning zeal, persecuting the church . . . " (v. 6) and being pleased with the consistency of his life-style: "touching the righteousness which is in the law, blameless . . . " (v. 6).

Nobody is going to knock heritage. It's good to know your catechism and your church history and to be proud of both. Unless, of course, you have such pride in this knowledge that the necessity of personal commitment to Jesus Christ eludes you. Then you're in trouble. Catechism didn't die on Calvary, and church history didn't rise again for you. Jesus did.

Enthusiasm is commendable in all people. There are so many pessimists around that a good old enthusiast is a delight—unless, of course, he is enthusiastically wrong.

Then he has problems and is a problem.

And consistency in life-style is to be encouraged, too. Or at least the consistency is to be encouraged; but the validity of the life-style is to be evaluated. And consistency to an invalid life-style doesn't make it miraculously valid.

Paul discovered all this when he found Christ. As a result, he was extremely leery of anything that might cloud the necessity for commitment to and trust in Jesus Christ. He realized how justly proud of his heritage and his life-style and his religion he had been until he saw to his horror that all of them ruled out Christ. But now, convinced that Christ was the truth, he knew that trust in anything that ruled out Christ was trust in a shaky substance, and commitment to a tottering cause.

Our problem, so often, is that we put our confidence in what we know and what we do and where we're going and what we plan. But if it rules out the Lord, it's the flesh. Some Christians have this delightful distinctive: they don't fall into the trap of trust in any of these areas. Christ is supreme in them!

Take a few minutes now to check on the realities of your spiritual experience. Are you realistic about your delight and your dangers and your distinctives?

Questions for Discussion

1. Have your ears, lips, and hearts been "circumcised" in an effort to be more responsive to God's will?

2. In what ways has the church become more interested in ritual than in reality? How can this attitude be combatted?

3. Are you a member of the circumcision or the concision?

4. What is the difference between a Christian's reality and the Christian religion?

5. Do you truly enjoy the Lord? How can you learn to enjoy or appreciate Him more?

6. Does your worship emphasize the spiritual over the physical, emotional, intellectual, and aesthetic? What role does each play in true worship of the Lord?

9

GETTING TO KNOW CHRIST BETTER

Yea doubtless, and I count all things but loss for the excellency of the knowledge of Christ Jesus my Lord: for whom I have suffered the loss of all things, and do count them but dung, that I may win Christ, and be found in him, not having mine own righteousness, which is of the law, but that which is through the faith of Christ, the righteousness which is of God by faith: That I may know him, and the power of his resurrection, and the fellowship of his sufferings, being made conformable unto his death; if by any means I might attain unto the resurrection of the dead.

Philippians 3:8-11

When the little boy fell out of bed and his mother asked how it happened, he replied, "I stayed too near where I got in." That's exactly how it is with many people in their spiritual experience. Satisfied that their sins are forgiven and that their reservations for heaven have been confirmed, they stay "where they got in." This is a sure way to spiritual boredom and ineffectiveness.

Paul could never be accused of settling for where he got in! His life was revolutionized through getting to know Christ, and he recognized that his knowledge was minimal compared to all that there was to know.

A Better Knowledge of Christ's Person

All relationships have to start somewhere, but they are expected to go somewhere, too. A relationship can be either tenuous and temporary or deep and intimate. When people engage in name dropping, the immediate thing we want to know is how well does the "dropper" know the "dropped." A Christian is a name dropper supreme. He drops the name above every name every time he uses the word "Christian," but the important thing is how well he really knows Christ.

Paul felt that the greatest thing that ever happened to him was getting to know Christ. "I count all things but loss for the excellency of the knowledge of Christ Jesus my Lord" (v. 8). The "all things" are all the things for which and by which he formerly lived.

Knowing Christ was totally radical and revolutionary to Paul. It changed everything. But note that the most important aspiration he had was to get to know Christ better: "That I may know him, and the power of his resurrection, and the fellowship of his sufferings" (v. 10). In short, Paul says that the greatest thing that ever happened to him was knowing Christ, and the greatest thing that is going to happen to him during his lifetime is getting to know Christ better.

Knowing Christ has two initial stages: preparatory knowledge and personal knowledge. Preparatory knowledge is knowing about Christ; knowing about His existence, His validity and His relevance.

That Jesus Christ existed is a historically verifiable fact accepted by all but the totally hardhearted. But having said that, we must realize that His historical existence raises some severe problems, for He made stupendous claims that need to be examined. In brief, He claimed to be the unique Son of God, the only way to the Father, the visible expression of an invisible God, and the final judge of the human race.

There are only two possible responses to these claims. Either He was right in making them, or He was wrong. If He was wrong, He was presumably trying to mislead people or He Himself was misled. If He was misleading, He was a crook, and if He was misled, He was a kook. So there are clear issues confronting the person convinced of the historical existence of Jesus of Nazareth. Was He Christ, was He a crook, or was He a kook?

But suppose a person accepts the existence and validity of Christ and says, "I believe that Jesus of Nazareth was the unique Son of God, but so what?" What happens then? That person needs to take a further step of knowledge about Christ to see the relevance of Christ to his own life. If Christ was the unique Son of God who died and rose again, He did it to provide forgiveness for sinners and power for living. The historic Christ of impeccable claims is relevant because through His work He can meet the needs of men and women in every succeeding century.

However, a person thus convinced still has to go further to *know* Christ. He must make the transition from preparatory knowledge to personal knowledge. The clue to this is found in two words that Paul uses: "my Lord." Note it is not "the Lord" or "everybody's Lord," but "*my* Lord." That is personal.

Intellectual conviction concerning the person, work and claims of Christ leads inevitably to moral demand. If Jesus is Lord in my thinking, He needs to be Lord in my acting. If He is Saviour in my convictions, He must save me in my sin. This requires the response of faith and the act of trust. It's like boarding an airplane. Intellectual conviction that it is really an airplane, that it can fly and that it is going to London is necessary, but inadequate as far as getting to London is concerned. Your intellectual conviction demands that you commit yourself to the object of your conviction. You must get on the airplane.

So it is with Christ. You take the step of acting on what you know, and you know that He will act on what He promised. You submit and commit your life to Him, and He will transmit His life and His Lordship to you. Then you can say, "I know Christ, He is *my* Lord."

Many things happen through the relationship that is born this way. Paul lists some of them. He got a new perspective: "I count all *things* but loss . . . " (v. 8); and a new position: "found in Him" (v. 9); and a new possession: "the righteousness which is of God" (v. 9). All that we have explained so far is little more than an introduction to Christ, and it is only after the introduction has taken place that real growth of knowledge and experience can take place.

There are three words that I believe are important when it comes to getting to know anybody better.

Time

First, it is necessary to realize that *time* must be spent in the conscious presence of the Lord. Just as a marriage can only develop as the partners take time to get to know each other, so your relationship with Christ requires the investment of time. Take time every day to get to know Christ better. But how?

All that we know of Christ historically and theologically

comes from the Bible. Experientially, we know Him through acts of obedience and faith, but these are acts that are responsive to what we have learned in the Word of God. Therefore, a basic rule of taking time to get to know Christ is to take time in your Bible daily in order to learn more of Him. This will require discipline and determination, but it must be done if your knowledge of Him is to grow.

Don't make the mistake of confusing knowledge of the Bible with knowing Christ. Knowledge of the Bible is intellectual; it must be translated into the experimental before it is knowledge of Christ. The experimental comes through response to what you learn from the Scriptures. There are some people who have little experience of Christ, not because they don't know their Bibles, but because they don't respond to what they know in order that Christ might be real to them.

For example, the Lord said, "Ye shall know the truth, and the truth shall make you free" (John 8:32). Now it is possible to know the truth of the emancipating power of the risen Lord without knowing liberty from sin, which is the whole point of knowing the truth of His power.

Faith in His working and obedience to His prompting will translate technical knowledge into the actual experience. Then Christ is known, not as One who is the truth that sets free, but as the One who actually sets you free, every time you trust Him and obey Him. Therefore, the more you spend time in the Book learning about Him, the more you can spend time experiencing in your body the things that you learned in His Book. And all the experience will be experience of Him.

Talk

"Talk" refers, of course, to communication with Him in prayer. The prayer life of a Christian is so important that its value can hardly be exaggerated even when it is described as "the Christian's vital breath." It is really that important.

When marriages go wrong, one of the first things to go is communication. The partners stop talking to each other and either freeze into silence or boil over into shouting. You don't get to know Christ better by silent discounting of Him or by shouting at Him, but by talking to Him.

Personally, I have found that my reading of the Scriptures leads me to talk with Him about what I've read. "Lord, I don't understand that," or "Lord, I don't like that," or sometimes, "Lord, that's new. Thank you for that." Each time I talk to Him, whether in the quiet of my study or driving to the hospital, flying in a jet or jogging in the early morning, I find the relationship grows, and my consciousness of His presence deepens.

Perhaps one of the reasons for this is that, as I talk to Him of my most intimate feelings, I am laying bare to my own consciousness the reality of my own being. What is more important, I am admitting the reality of what I am and what I have done to the One who really matters. This is so helpful, for if I either refuse to admit the reality of my being or fail to admit it to Him, I will gradually degenerate into an unreal person living in a fool's paradise. Talking to Him and taking time with Him not only lets me get to know Him, but it helps me to know me!

Trust

If we are to get to know what a person is made of and what they are capable of doing, trust is all-important. How often we determine that a person is incapable of doing something for no other reason than that we have never seen him or her do it! And sometimes the only reason he or she has never been seen doing it is that we never gave him or her the opportunity. This is especially true of young people. They are written off as "irresponsible" when they have never been given responsibility. They are regarded as "untrustworthy" without anybody counting them worthy of trust.

Some people never learn of Christ's faithfulness because they never put themselves in a position where they are dependent solely on His faithfulness. They never experience the might of His power because their lives are run on the basis of their own ability to do whatever needs doing. They don't need much evidence of the supernatural because they live exclusively in the arena of the natural.

Many Christians never need to trust Christ for anything until tragedy hits them, for their Christianity is so mundane and predictable that it takes nothing more than halfhearted commitment and tiny drops of perspiration to accomplish it. They are like children in the shallow end of the pool who fake swimming while keeping their feet on the bottom. General appearances are good, but practical experience of the strange buoyancy of water is negligible.

Christ made it clear that many reckless initiatives should be taken in His name. "Go ye into all the world," "Launch out into the deep," "First be reconciled to your brother," "Give and it shall be given to you," "Lift up your eyes and look . . . . " Now all these imperatives, if obeyed, put people in a position of tension that can be met only through the person of the living Christ. If they never take these initiatives and obey these imperatives, they will survive in a Christian sub-culture, but they will neither know the exhilaration of triumph or discover the faithfulness and the ability of Christ.

It takes trust to release trustworthiness and faith to realize faithfulness, and without these things in the Christian life, a Christian can never learn personally these aspects of Christ's person. So what Paul is saying is, "I'm going to go on talking and trusting and spending time with my Lord, knowing full well that as I do I will get to know Him more and more as the days go by."

A Better Knowledge of Christ's Power

"That I may know him, and the power of his resurrection . . . " (v. 10). It is interesting to see how the different writers of the New Testament expressed the same truths in different ways. John talked about people being born again, Matthew saw them as members of a kingdom, Peter thought of them as having come into a new inheritance, and Paul loved to talk about them being risen from the dead. They were all making the same point.

A person who comes to a personal experience of Christ has a totally new sphere of existence through his relationship to Christ. He is born through the new life of Christ, who is King of the kingdom into which he has been born. As a result, he is heir to an incorruptible inheritance that is so different from anything he previously experienced that it is like being raised from the deadness of the old life into the freshness and newness of a new life.

All this is possible through Christ. The better He is known the greater will be the growth of the new baby, the more effective will be the resident of the heavenly kingdom, the more fully will the inheritance be appreciated and the greater will be the impact of the resurrected person.

So Paul is intent on knowing more of the power of resurrection. It should be noted that the basis of the message preached by the early church was the resurrected Christ. That He had risen from the dead and ascended into heaven was the ground of their hope and thrust of their message. Men and women had seen the risen Lord. The disciples had watched His ascent into heaven. They knew these things were true.

But Paul had much more in his mind when he talked of knowing the power of resurrection. In his theology, once a person committed himself to Christ he identified with Christ in everything. He died with Christ to all that Christ died to; he regarded himself as thoroughly buried to his pre-Christian life as Christ was buried at the termination of His earthly life. But more than that, Paul insisted that a Christian was raised to a new life as completely as Christ was raised by the power of the Spirit from the depths of the grave.

All these things had essentially practical connotations in Paul's thinking. "If ye then be risen with Christ, seek those thing which are above" (Col. 3:1). Seeking higher living is the practical result of co-resurrection. "How shall we, that are dead [in Christ] to sin, live any longer therein?" (Rom. 6:2). Co-crucifixion results in antipathy to anything that caused Christ's crucifixion.

Paul wanted his own life and the lives of other believers to reflect in practical, everyday living the wonders of resurrection power. How do you release the power in your life? You start with God's source book, the Bible.

Take a look in the Word concerning some of your present longings. See what God has to say about your temper or your jealousy or your laziness. Does He condemn these things? If He does, He expects you to finish with them. Do you want to be done with them because you are related to Christ? Good, then the resources are within you in resurrection proportions. Now you can act on these resources. Tell the Lord you believe Him, and you will obey Him. Then do what He said, and things will happen.

A Better Knowledge of Christ's Passion

"That I may know him, and the power of his resurrection, and the fellowship of his sufferings, being made conformable unto His death" (v. 10). This gives the balance to the whole truth. There is no shortage of people in the world today who are longing for a "closer walk" or a "deeper commitment." And there is no shortage of man-made answers to these expressed needs. However, there is one thing that is distressingly common in many of these answers, and that is the absence of any idea of cost or suffering involved. We can understand this when we realize how selective many people are in their reading of the Word, and when we ponder the instant theories of growth that so many people find acceptable. But when we look at Scripture, we find no room for a painless commitment.

There is no resurrection without a crucifixion. No cross, no empty tomb. It takes a cross to fill the tomb in order to give resurrection a chance to empty it. There is no way out of this aspect of knowing Christ. "Know Me," says Christ. "Know My suffering." Peter and Paul didn't always see eye-to-eye, but they did on this. Peter put it this way: "Beloved, think it not strange concerning the fiery trial . . . but rejoice, inasmuch as ye are partakers of Christ's sufferings" (1 Pet. 4:12,13). And Paul had been reared spiritually on the words that Ananias brought to him on the day his eyes were opened: "I will shew him how great things he must suffer for my name's sake" (Acts 9:16).

This might sound strangely like, "Good news for modern masochists," but it is not intended to. Rather, it is designed to show the depth of identification that is necessary for vibrant Christian experience.

A quick glance at the things of Christ suffered and the reasons for the suffering should clarify any muddled thinking. Christ suffered the attacks of Satan; fellowship with Christ's suffering will open the Christian to possible attacks in this area. In hell's game plan, sleeping saints are allowed to lie; but once they wake up they are targets for attack. Christ suffered ostracism from man. So great was it that finally they crucified Him. Christ didn't make "Man of the Year" in *Time* magazine, but He makes it every year in heaven. So a certain amount of ostracism is to be expected if identification really takes place. It's strange how warm hearts can result in the cold shoulder!

Christ also suffered for the redemption of the lost. I see no way in which a person can have a deep spirituality without having a commitment to evangelism, and that means all kinds of suffering in terms of time and prayer and money and sheer down-to-earth involvement. There is no shortcut to knowing Christ's person, Christ's power and His passion. It's a long road that ends in heaven, and then, and then only, we will know as we are known. (See 1 Cor. 13:12.)

Questions for Discussion

1. How well do you know the One whose name you drop every time you call yourself a Christian?

2. How do sufferings help us to know Christ better? What images come to mind when you hear that Christians have fellowship in sharing Christ's sufferings?

3. What is your response to the following statement? "Knowing Christ is like believing in a bullet-proof vest. It's one thing to believe the vest can save your life; but it's another matter completely to put the vest on and ask someone to shoot you."

4. If someone were to "bug" your prayer closet, what would be heard? What might someone assume about your relationship to Christ, based upon what was heard?

10

FOLLOW ME

Not as though I had already attained, either were already perfect: but I follow after, if that I may apprehend that for which also I am apprehended of Christ Jesus. Brethren, I count not myself to have apprehended: but this one thing I do, forgetting those things which are behind, and reaching forth unto those things which are before, I press toward the mark for the prize of the high calling of God in Christ Jesus. Let us therefore, as many as be perfect, be thus minded: and if in any thing ye be otherwise minded, God shall reveal even this unto you. Nevertheless, whereto we have already attained, let us walk by the same rule, let us mind the same thing. Brethren, be followers together of me, and mark them which walk so as ye have us for an ensample. (For many walk, of whom I have told you often, and now tell you even weeping, that they are the enemies of the cross of Christ: whose end is destruction, whose God is their belly, and whose glory is in their shame, who mind earthly things.) For our conversation is in heaven; from whence also we look for the Saviour, the Lord Jesus Christ: who shall change our vile body, that it may be fashioned like unto his glorious body, according to the working whereby he is able even to subdue all things unto himself.

Philippians 3:12-21

Christians have a unique role to play. They are intended to be "earth people," which they are by birth, and "heaven people," which they are by new birth, both at the same time. This means that they are people of two realms living in one of those realms. Their role is to tell the realm where they live what the other realm is like. Their "conversation is in heaven." (v. 20), which means that they are citizens of heaven, but they live on earth to bring a touch of heaven wherever they go.

This sounds rather delightful, and it certainly is, but it also has problems for the Christian who tries to function in this manner. The main difficulty is that earth operates in a totally different manner from heaven. If the Christian isn't careful, he can become so involved with the philosophies of the world where he lives that instead of bringing heaven to earth, he lets earth rob him of his enjoyment of heaven. Paul is keenly aware of this and warns his people of the dangers that confront them. He cites the dangers of being governed by purely sensual appetites ("whose god is their belly"—the "eat, drink and be merry" group philosophy). There is plenty of evidence that contemporary Christians have been infected by this approach to life.

Then there is the danger of material obsession ("who mind earthly things"). The insidious disease of materialism is possibly one of the most chronic ailments of the contemporary church. Notice carefully what Paul says. His thesis is that those who are governed by sensual appetites and material obsession are also the "enemies of the cross" who "glory in their shame" and whose "end is destruction." Is there any way in which a Christian can explain how his life-style can fit in with those people? Of course not. But what can he do if he finds that it is happening? Paul makes a startling statement at this juncture which, if not seen in context, would appear to be rank arrogance. He says, "Brethren, be followers together of me" (v. 17).

His point here is not to put himself on a pedestal, but

to give them an example of Christian living that is as real
and practical as the practical living that is influencing them.
In other words, he says, "Don't copy the example of your
pagan neighbor. Copy me. I'm a citizen of heaven like you.
He isn't." We need this kind of example today. Christians
do not always fulfill the beautiful role of being the transmit-
ters of "heaven's life-style" to an earth that is becoming
increasingly confused. I'm afraid that society is infecting
the church to a greater extent than the church is affecting
society.

Let us look at Paul's life-style as he explains it, and see
in what ways he needs to be accepted as an example by us
today. Life-style is a reflection of philosophy. The
"swinger" swings because of a certain mental attitude
toward life; the radical acts radically because of radical
convictions; the conservative seeks to conserve that
which he is convinced ought to be conserved. The Christian life-style is firmly linked to Christian philosophy or
outlook.

Paul gives us four aspects of his outlook which help us
to understand his behavior and, accordingly, give us a concrete example to follow.

He Takes a Backward Look

One day he was "apprehended of Christ Jesus," (v.
12), and he never forgot it. *Apprehend* means *to seize and
take possession of,* and that is exactly what he thought
Christ had done to him. Christ had stopped him in his furi-
ous pursuit of error, and had delivered him from the consequences of his own arrogant refusal to listen to the claims
of Christ. Not that Christ had stopped him dead in his
tracks. It was more like putting the brakes on little by little.

Paul could look back over his life and see how the Lord
had been putting on the brakes. There was the impact of

the Christian message of the Resurrection, which we can be sure Paul would have refuted if he could. I am sure that he had spent long hours investigating the whole story trying to find a loophole in it. Years afterward he was able to say, "If Christ is not risen our faith is vain." I am certain he worked on that thesis in his Pharisee days. He tried to invalidate the Christian message by disproving the Resurrection, but he couldn't.

Then there was the obstinate refusal of the Christians to be intimidated, their insistence on defying the authorities, their insistence that "We ought to obey God rather than men" (Acts 5:29).

Stephen shattered him, for as Paul stood guard over the jackets of the stone throwers, he saw Stephen with angelic face praying for those who were killing him. He heard him exclaim, "I see . . . the Son of man standing on the right hand of God" (Acts 7:56), and saw him die in triumph.

Then there was the vision on the road, and then the final pressure of the brakes as Ananias came, laid his hands on Paul and called him, "Brother." That was too much. Christ had stopped him. He was arrested by Christ Jesus.

Of course, Christ didn't stop him for the sake of stopping him. He stopped him to save him; and anyone reading anything written by Paul will understand the immensity of his understanding of "salvation." It was a doctrine of emancipation from anything and everything that keeps a man or woman from being what God intended them to be. He learned immediately of salvation, but also saw that his salvation would be complete only when Christ took him to glory. In the interim he anticipated countless "salvation" experiences. Christ stopped him, saved him and then started him all over again in a totally new direction, to be what he had never been, to do what he had never done. He was possessed by Christ Jesus, and he often looked back to the day of his arrest.

There was another thing that he did about the past, "Forgetting those thing which are behind" (v. 13), did not mean that he never thought of his old life and what he had been saved from, but it meant that he did not dwell on the defeats of victories of past days. He was alert to the fact that every day has to be lived in the strength of that day made available through the Lord of each day.

This is a timely lesson. So often people try to live on the traditions of the past or the memories of the good old days. Years ago I was preaching in South Wales, and wherever I went I heard tales of the "Welsh Revival." The stories were exciting, but not terribly relevant. There was an obvious need to live in the "now" and forget about the "then," because it almost appeared that the glories of the "good old days" were being accepted as valid substitutes for what should have been the glories of "today." It didn't seem to matter very much that nothing was happening, because it had happened once!

Then there are those people who are so mortified by the old days and so conscious of their gross failure and sin that they are totally impotent in the present. If you are ridden with guilt you don't really understand justification. To be justified is to be cleared in the courts of heaven and to know that all is forgiven, all charges have been met, all sin has been judged, and the defendant is as pure as the driven snow in the eyes of the judge. To believe that God has forgiven you, and yet not forgive yourself, is to put yourself in a position superior to God. If He forgave you, you'd better forgive yourself and "forget those things which are behind."

So there we have it. A backward look that helps us understand the man who tells us to use him as an example. He's conscious of having been stopped, saved and started all over again. The past is past, and the present is here, and that is where he lives.

He Takes an Upward Look

Christians have often been accused of being so heavenly minded that they are no earthly use. But I feel that isn't really the problem. On the contrary, I believe we are so earthly minded we are no heavenly use. We are like the man in Bunyan's *Pilgrim's Progress* "that could look no way but downwards with a muckrake in his hand." If a Christian is to fulfill his unique role on earth, it is vital that he should be so in tune with heaven that he can interpret heaven to earthlings. Like Paul, he needs the upward look.

A Heavenly Goal

The word *mark* means a *goal on which to fix your attention.* Christians all too often settle for lesser goals than the heavenly one of "the high calling of God." Their lives have been so earthbound that, like the man with the muckrake, they are oblivious to the angel hovering overhead with the crown. There is no crown for our activity if it is unrelated to the goal of presenting everything to Him who sits on the throne.

A Heavenly Prize

This expression Paul borrows from the Roman games. The *prize* is the reward given by the umpires to the winners of athletic events. Like all athletes, Paul is prepared to forego certain things that appear attractive and may be perfectly legitimate, so that he may win the prize. I have always been challenged by the dedication of athletes that will keep them running the wet streets of dismal cities night after night in order that they might have a crack at an Olympic gold medal four years later.

Paul sees a similarity between the athlete and the Christian in the area of purposefulness and dedication. So it is not hard to see how he could get many things into perspective that would otherwise be vague and fuzzy. Suffering doesn't seem half as insufferable if there's a prize. Hardship is nowhere near as hard if there is reward. Loss of material blessings that are temporal is so much easier to take in the light of spiritual blessings that are eternal. So he thinks of a prize.

A Heavenly Call

The "heavenly call" is literally the *upward call* of God. This can mean two things. It is an upward call because it originated up there where God reigns supreme, and it is upward because that is the direction it will take the Christian. To believe that you are called from the throne of heaven to be heaven's representative on earth does something to any thoughtful Christian. To know that your call will not be rescinded, and will only be terminated when you finally arrive up there, is comforting. Take the challenge of it, mix it with the comfort of it and live in the light of the upward call. It will constantly militate against the downward drag. Some people find Christians hard to take because they just don't fit into the right kind of mold. They don't understand that Christians have substituted downward drag for upward call and, accordingly, are heading in the opposite direction.

A Heavenly Lord

Paul speaks of heaven as the place of the Christian's citizenship, and adds, "from whence also we look for the Saviour, the Lord Jesus Christ" (v. 20). The world of Paul's day was teetering on the edge of disaster. There was unrest and decadence, obscenity and injustice. Cruelty and violence were facts of life, and the very structures of society were shaking. This may sound like today's world, and it is.

Paul fully expected a divine intervention in the affairs of men during his lifetime. He looked for the return of Christ to claim His true possession and establish His eternal kingdom. Paul welcomed the thought and dwelt on it greatly. Since Paul's day, generation after generation has seen society's structure shaken and world danger increasing. Each generation has looked for the Lord to intervene. What can we say about our day? Many things have been said and are being said with varying degrees of dogmatism and sensationalism. Suffice it to say that His coming is as certain today as it was in Paul's day, it is as vitally necessary today as it was then, and it is approximately 2000 years nearer. So look up, "the coming of the Lord draweth nigh" (Jas. 5:8).

A Heavenly Ultimate

The Lord Paul expects to return is going to "change our vile body, that it may be fashioned like unto his glorious body . . . " (v. 21). Paul insists that the ultimate life is a spirit alive to the living Lord and inhabiting a resurrection body like the Lord's. Glory unspeakable is the ultimate of Paul's understanding of salvation, and that affects his lifestyle down here. What you believe about the sweet by-and-by should always have repercussions on what you do in the tough here-and-now. An upward look and a backward look will keep you in line with God's plan for your life.

An Inward Look

There is danger in looking backward and upward, the danger of being so extroverted that you become careless of your present state and oblivious to your immediate responsibilities. That is why a mature experience demands the inward look to balance the other two. As Paul carefully examines his own life, he admits, "not as though I had already attained, either were already perfect . . . " (v. 12). This is encouraging to me, particularly as I become increasingly aware of my own immaturity, and as I meet people who insist or imply that they *have* arrived. These people are ahead of the apostle Paul, so he can't be an example to them. But he's a great help to me, so I let them go on their confused way while I take heart from him. He has not managed to be all that he knows God wants of him; he readily admits that there is much to be done.

This is important, because people who tell you that they have reached a stage of development that leaves little or nothing to be done in their lives are forgetting things. First, the Christian life is growth, and to stop growing is not biblical. It is not a sign of maturity, but of arrested development. Second, spiritual growth has as its goal "the measure of the stature of the fulness of Christ" (Eph. 4:13), and to say that you are there or even approaching it is dangerous thinking and talking. Better stand with Paul and say, "There is so much to be done."

Personally, I go along with the hymn which says,

> "They who fain would serve Him best
> Are conscious most of wrong within."

Now this is not intended to be a plug for those who are satisfied with *no* growth, who say, "Well, I never will be like Him this side of glory. I'm only human, so what can you expect, particularly when you bear in mind my circumstances, my heritage and my ulcer." By no means. A maturing Christian is not satisfied with his present growth, and he or she desires to deal with what is wrong and to discover what is not known.

The expression, "either were already perfect" (v. 12), when coupled with, "Let us therefore, as many as be perfect" (v. 15), sounds suspiciously like double talk. The idea of perfection in our minds has the connotation of "absence of evil and devoid of flaw," but this is not the meaning here. *Perfect* means *mature or complete*. Paul is not inconsistent when he says, "I'm not complete when I realize that the ultimate completeness is Christlikeness, but I am complete in the sense that I have grown as far as I can at the present, and I am ready for the next lesson." In other words, completeness and maturity are relative to the completeness of Christ, and that completeness is accomplished only in glory; but on the way there should be growth in Christlikeness in relation to what you know at any one time.

A Forward Look

In the midst of all the heavenly looks and the introspective evaluations of Christlikeness, it is good to note the forward look. There are two expressions that we must note. First, "I follow after . . . " (v. 12), and, second, "I press toward the mark . . . " (v. 14). At first sight there appears to be no connection between the two, but they are different translations of the same Greek word. It means *to pursue,* but even that does not give the full meaning that Paul wants to convey. The word is also translated *persecute* in other places, and so we could say that he means *to pursue relentlessly,* which is what a persecutor does. What is he pursuing relentlessly? All that we have talked about up till now. They are not abstract ideas; they are principles of belief that he relentlessly interprets into action. The degree of intensity must not be missed. He isn't treating his Christian experience like a Sunday stroll in the park, but as a race to be run with relentless determination and commitment.

The picture is strengthened by another expression that he uses: "reaching forth unto . . . " (v. 13), which means *to stretch out* and probably is an analogy taken from the sprints that were so popular in the games of Paul's day. It is easy for those who have seen "Wide World of Sports" to know what he means. We have seen the sprinters neck and neck heading for the tape and diving, stretching those last few yards. That's the expression he uses.

So Paul has a philosophy that he interprets into action which becomes his life-style. We can take it as a matter of academic interest, or we can do what he says about it. Instead of being influenced and infected by a world that is hostile and apathetic to Christ and His kingdom, we should be motivated to live as resident aliens on earth, and, if we need an example, Paul gives us one: himself! He says, "Imitate me and those who walk in similar fashion."

Questions for Discussion

1. Are there signs of a growing materialism in your church? What can be done to change this focus?

2. In what ways is the Christian emancipated from bondage? In what ways does a Christian willingly become a slave? How are freedom and slavery compatible in the Christian life?

3. What are the main events in the Christian's olympics? How can we best prepare for competition?

4. Are you satisfied with the level of Christian maturity which you have reached? What will you do to call a halt to that complacency?

5. What are you pursuing in life? Is your pursuit of Christian maturity a relentless one?

11

ALL-AROUND LIVING

Therefore, my brethren dearly beloved and longed for, my joy and crown, so stand fast in the Lord, my dearly beloved. I beseech Euodias, and beseech Syntyche, that they be of the same mind in the Lord. And I entreat thee also, true yokefellow, help those women which labored with me in the gospel, with Clement also, and with other my fellow laborers, whose names are in the book of life. Rejoice in the Lord always: and again I say, Rejoice. Let your moderation be known unto all men. The Lord is at hand. Be careful for nothing; but in every thing by prayer and supplication with thanksgiving let your requests be made known unto God. And the peace of God, which passeth all understanding, shall keep you hearts and minds through Christ Jesus.

Philippians 4:1-7

Life can be so unpredictable. You just never know what is going to happen next. When you think you have everything exactly as you want it, something that you don't want comes along, and it's time to start all over again. At least there is no time to be bored!

The unpredictability of life is due in part to the unpredictable people we meet, the unpredictable problems we face and the unpredictable situations we encounter. But I have good news for you. The Scriptures give us guidelines that tell us how to cope with the people, the problems and the situations that come our way.

Obviously, it is not possible for the Bible to tell us exactly what to do in every minute situation. "If your baby swallows the drain cleaner, and the dog is sick on the carpet, while the phone is ringing in the den, and the electric blanket has caught fire in the master bedroom, and Junior has driven the new car through the garage doors, first do this, then this, and so on!" No, it doesn't deal with the specifics of that kind of situation because, as you will agree, there is an infinite number of variations possible on the theme of household disaster! But it does deal in principles which cover just about everything.

How to Greet Every Situation

The principle is, "Rejoice in the Lord always" (v. 4), and the word that I want you to note very carefully is *always*. That word is all-inclusive. It covers every eventuality and in principle tells you what to do with every situation. This idea is not without its difficulties. There are some aspects of it that are not easy to understand or to do when they are understood.

A careful reading of the instruction will show that it does not say, "Rejoice always." That would be ludicrous, cruel and totally unrealistic. *In the Lord* is what makes it different from any other instruction of this nature that you may have heard. The term *in the Lord* appears in "stand fast in the Lord" (v. 1), and "be of the same mind in the Lord" (v. 2), in addition to the occasion that we are considering in verse 4. Obviously, therefore, it is much more than a pious phrase or an ecclesiastical cliché.

Paul is concerned that his disciples in Philippi be able to survive the onslaughts of opposition that he is convinced are coming their way. He wants them to *stand,* and he says they can and must do it *in the Lord.* The phrase, therefore, has something to tell us concerning the ability that Christians have to do what is not natural to them in their own ability. Standing *in the Lord* makes people who *can't stand* up to some things *stand* up to them.

Then in the case of Euodias and Syntyche there is a fervent request that they get off each other's backs and get on with the business in hand. To be told, "Be of the same mind in the Lord," not only gives the impression that there is power *in the Lord* to do what normally would not be done, but also that behavior is expected of those *in the Lord* that cannot be expected of those not *in the Lord.* To summarize then, *in the Lord* is a sphere of spiritual experience wherein lie unusual resources of strength and unusual expectations of behavior.

There are some circumstances in which people are not going to be deliriously happy. People not *in the Lord* in those situations simply aren't very happy, and that's all there is to it! But people *in the Lord* have reserves of strength that allow them to be above their circumstances and to live in an area of existence where supranormal behavior is expected. Hence the instruction, "Rejoice in the Lord always."

But the big question that arises is, "How can you rejoice in the Lord when your circumstances and situations are not conducive to joy and rejoicing?" Before we try to answer that question, it is important that we note that Paul was not talking theoretically at this point. In verse 10 he says, "But I rejoiced in the Lord greatly . . . " This rejoicing happened in an experience where he had been neglected by his friends for some time and had suffered severely from loneliness and depression. But still he rejoiced in the Lord!

The first part of the answer lies in the title *Lord*. This superb name given to Jesus of Nazareth speaks of His sovereign majesty, mighty power and controlling mastery of the universe. As we saw earlier, one day every knee will bow to Him and every tongue confess that He is Lord.

The believer who really believes this, is a believer who really believes that the Lord is Lord. There are countless believers who have problems believing and many who confess a Lord who is apparently something less than Lord. Any person who believes (that is, *trusts*) in the Lord (that is, *the Supreme One*) really trusts the Supreme One. And anyone who trusts the Supreme One has no alternative but to trust His supremacy when situations appear that apparently challenge that supremacy.

The second part of the answer is found in the words *in the Lord*. This may appear to be splitting hairs, but I assure you it is not. Numerous phrases are used in Scripture to describe the relationship existing between a believer and the Lord. This one, *in the Lord,* speaks of being brought into His Body by the Spirit and the resultant identification of the believer in the eternal purposes and destiny of the Lord. This at once brings thoughts of security to the believer's mind. *In Christ,* he is identified with Him in His destiny, as secure as He and and as sure as He. It also means that as the believer is so completely related to Christ as to be regarded as being in *Him,* so Christ is totally related to the believer as to be regarded as being *in* the believer.

Even a passing glance at this angle of divine truth will reveal depths of possibilities that boggle the imagination. Suffice it to say at this juncture that the person who is *in the Lord* is secure, sure and strong through this relationship. Therefore, he should rejoice in his position and relate to his possession of strength.

When this is clear in a person's mind he is then required to be obedient to the command, *Rejoice*. This requires an act of the will based on the understanding of the mind. But a word of caution may be necessary here. To obey the command to rejoice does not mean to ignore the situation in which you are to rejoice. I have met people who got so excited about this aspect of truth that they "rejoiced" in their dilemmas beautifully while their families went hungry.

To rejoice in the Lord does not mean to ignore your responsibilities, neither does it mean to evade obvious issues. Rather, it means to be fully cognizant of the situation, fully prepared to deal with it responsibly, and fully convinced of the power of the Lord to give you wisdom, grace and courage to deal with whatever comes along. When this attitude is adopted it will not produce a giddy irresponsibility or a naive ecstacy, but a deep, mature, responsible faith that has as its core a majestic Lord. When He is the One at the core, joy can result because of the certainty of His ultimate triumph, the assurance of His benevolent purpose and the opportunities for spiritual growth that the situation affords.

So there we have it. Not minute instructions on what to do with every daily disaster, but overall instructions on what to do in every situation. "Rejoice in the Lord always: and again I say, Rejoice."

How to Treat Every Person

Sometimes, of course, it isn't so much the situations that make our day but the people we meet during the day. They can be difficult! The Word of God does not ignore this fact; it gives explicit instructions on what to do about it.

While Scripture does not deal with specifics, it certainly lays down basic, enduring, binding principles. "Let your moderation be known unto all men" (v. 5). Having just considered the *always* of rejoicing, note carefully the *all men* of relating. The principle is all-encompassing in terms of people-problems as the previous principle was all-embracing in situational difficulties.

One of the magnificent doctrines of the Bible has to do with the solidarity of the human race. All people are created by God, for God, to live before God and answer to God. In this we are one. All people were made in the image of God; all were marred by the fall of Adam. In this we are one. All people have a fallen nature and a lost condition, and all are spiritually dead. In this we are one. All people are loved of God, have a need of salvation and many find it in Christ. In this we are one.

Biologically we are one because we are interfertile. Geographically we are one because we inhabit a desperately frail little planet. Socially we are one because we cannot survive without mutual cooperation. Physically we are one because we are made of identical elements and return to identical dust. Intellectually we are one, for we can learn each other's languages and communicate each other's ideas.

Mankind is one. But who would ever believe it? Communists hate capitalists and capitalists distrust Communists. The "haves" have what the "have nots" have not. The "have nots" want what the "haves" have, and the "haves" have no intention of letting them have it. Whites have oppressed blacks, and blacks think it is time to get even with whites. Arabs and Jews come from the same stock, and there the oneness ends. Women regard men as "chauvinist pigs," and men return the compliment by regarding women as sex objects. Youth despises authority and authority clobbers youth. And on and on it goes. But mankind is one!

Somewhere along the line the biblical doctrine of mankind has to emerge for the well-being of all. It hasn't been heard too much recently, and the reason is plain to see. The voice of the Word, the church of Jesus Christ, has become embroiled in the hassles of fragmented society and is no longer able to speak with any degree of conviction to the subject of "all men." But individual Christians who may feel that they themselves cannot change anything must realize that they can and must. They must "let their moderation be known to all men." That would help tremendously!

But what does it mean? *Moderation* is a word that has worried me for a long time. It always sounded insipid. Neither hot nor cold, but lukewarm. I didn't want to be moderate when there were so many things around that needed changing radically. I would rather be radical than moderate! But there were so many truths and institutions that were of God and had to be conserved that I wanted to be conservative and contend for the faith! In fact, I wanted to be anything but moderate. Then I studied the word. It means *forbearance,* and Matthew Arnold called it, "sweet reasonableness." And that's exactly what is needed!

That is what the Bible has to say about the Christian's treatment of all people. Immediately it rules out many of the time-honored attitudes for which the church has been known—its attitudes to the underprivileged and the impoverished, the unregenerate and the unreached. Whatever his or her color or creed, caste or conviction, a person is a person and as such is deserving of "sweet reasonableness" from a Christian.

What a thrill to be a Christian who sees only men and women for whom Christ died. To know only compassion for those whom Christ sought. What delight to be able to overlook everything in order to get the issues clearly in focus. This is no easy matter, but it is what the Word says, so that's the way it is.

Look at Paul's "moderation" showing. He talks of the

Philippians as "my brethren," "my joy" and "my crown," and "my dearly beloved." These are terms that are indicative of his feelings towards people. To regard people as brothers is quite different from seeing them as threats or viewing them as opponents. I realize that these expressions are addressed to Christians and have special Christian connotations, but the Christian meaning does not exhaust all possible meaning. There is a sense in which every man is brother to every man, whether or not he is brother in terms of new birth and Fatherhood of God. This is something we forget too easily.

To see people as a "joy" rather than as a victim for possible exploitation is another angle that would help contemporary society. People can be a nuisance and a bore. They can drive you to distraction and plunge you to despair. But still they can be a joy. Even the dispensers of despair and distraction!

So much depends on understanding the person concerned and analyzing your reactions to the person concerned. Why does he drive you up the wall and halfway across the ceiling? Is it because he is too demanding of your time when you have so many other people to see? Then tell him (with sweet reasonableness!), even if it hurts his feelings. Why does she plunge you to despair? Is it because she doesn't seem to get the message and never shows signs of improvement? Could it be that you aren't making yourself clear, or is it that she is unwilling to do what she knows she should? If it is your fault, try again to be clear. If it is hers, tell her so, and firmly inform her that you cannot spend your time working with people who don't cooperate. Even in the most trying circumstances "sweet reasonableness" should be operative. There is joy in people when they are treated correctly and handled God's way.

Make a careful note of *my crown,* for this gives a great clue to Paul's attitude towards people. The *crown* he refers to is yet another reference to the Olympic Games. It was not a crown of gold or a tiara of diamonds, but a wreath of leaves placed on the victor's head. To Paul, people were evidences of battles fought and victories won. Not Paul's personal battles, but battles in which God was honored and His purposes vindicated. Every redeemed soul was a leaf in his garland—a trophy of the victory of God.

There are innumerable opportunities for this kind of attitude. Look at all those potential leaves in a victor's crown that bustle past you in the subway and shout at football games and even watch television in your den.

But there is something else that even crowns the crown. "My dearly beloved" is repeated twice in one verse. Love is the key; and remember that God's love is not related to character or merit—just need. Then treat people on that basis.

How to Meet Every Problem

Some people are more prone to problems than others, in the same way that some are more susceptible to colds, but sooner or later everybody comes up with a problem. They vary in intensity and complexity. Some are trivial and others are what Sherlock Holmes called "a three pipe problem," which I suppose to the rest of us would be "practically insurmountable."

Some people make problems pay and others pay dearly for their problems. Whatever the situation, problems come and have to be dealt with. My wife says that my favorite expression is, "I don't anticipate any major problems," and she's probably right. In fact, she has told me that she will have engraved on my tombstone, "Here lies Stuart Briscoe; he didn't anticipate any major problems."

Joking apart, problems have to be met, and the Word says how it is to be done. "Be careful for nothing; but in every thing by prayer and supplication with thanksgiving let your requests be made known unto God" (v. 6). You will remember the *always* of rejoicing and the *all men* of relationships, and now note the *everything* of reaction. Every problem, large or small, is to be seen in its proper perspective and dealt with as this verse states.

First, "Be careful for nothing," does not mean "get careless and reckless about everything." This ought to be obvious when we see that Paul spoke with sorrow of the lack of care for the Philippians in the Roman church (Phil. 2:20). Care has a real place in Christian experience. To be anxious for people's well-being, and even your own, is permissible and admirable, but to stay in a state of chronic anxiety is to show that you are not doing with your anxiety what ought to be done. Anxiety in a Christian must elicit more than natural reaction, for in spiritual experience it is intended to stimulate prayer. What do you do with you anxieties?

There are a number of words used to describe the activities of prayer, but the first one used here is the most common. It always has to do with approaching God and, therefore, gives a sense of *worship and reverence.* Some people in foxholes have been known to pray "foxhole prayers," like the man who prayed, "God get me out of here, and I'll never bother you again." And he didn't! It is doubtful if that kind of praying has any validity whatsoever. The prayer which effectively presents problems to the Father is the prayer that sees the Father as God and treats Him with awe.

The second word, *supplications,* contains the thought of need and deep desire for the need to be met. It is sometimes translated *beseech.* It is apparent, therefore, that requests for answers to problems should be presented with a great degree of intensity. It would appear that God wants you to be serious about your problems if you want Him to deal with them seriously.

The third word, *thanksgiving,* conveys the idea of

gratitude. The person who has a problem will be as grateful for a God who hears prayers as a sick man in the jungle is grateful to find a doctor on the river bank. He will also be grateful for the fact that he can share the burden and know the concern of God's loving heart. On top of that, the Holy Spirit may assure him that God is acting positively on his request, and gratitude will fill his soul. It is quite clear that whatever we do with our problems we must not hesitate to speak to the Lord about them, making requests with a sense of reverence, intensity and gratitude.

There is one final thing that must be mentioned before we conclude this chapter. There is a superb promise for the problem-plagued soul that handles the problems God's way. The promise is, "And the peace of God, which passeth all understanding, shall keep your hearts and minds through Christ Jesus" (v. 7).

To *keep* does not mean to *retain,* but to act as a garrison of soldiers; to protect and defend and make an impregnable defense. That is what the peace of God can do. A few years ago I stood with the widow of one of my best friends who had just been killed in his airplane. She was smitten with grief, but spoke of peace, I reminded her of the "peace the passes all understanding," and she said, "I never realized what it meant, but I now know how it feels." It was a garrison to her mind, to maintain her mental equilibrium; and to her heart, to give her emotional stability.

Handled according to divine principles, the unpredictable things of life can become the means of the unexplainable peace of God acting as a garrison in our hearts and minds. This must be our experience as we meet the situations and the people and the problems that make up our daily lives.

Questions for Discussion

1. What is the difference between "rejoicing always" and "rejoicing in the Lord always"?

2. If Christian love is not related to character or merit, but to need, then to whom are we to give love? Is your love of the brethren directed only to those who "deserve" it? What of the needy around you?

3. Does your prayer life reflect the awesomeness of God? How do you worship God's majesty?

4. What does "the peace that passeth understanding" mean to you? Are you claiming that peace as you deal with the blessings and burdens of each day?

12
THINK AND DO

Finally, brethren, whatsoever things are true, whatsoever things are honest, whatsoever things are just, whatsoever things are pure, whatsoever things are lovely, whatsoever things are of good report; if there be any virtue, and if there be any praise, think on these things. Those things, which ye have both learned, and received, and heard, and seen in me, do; and the God of peace shall be with you.

Philippians 4:8,9

An old farmer was a little concerned about the boy who was working for him, so he asked him, "What do you do in your spare time, John?" John replied, "Sometimes I sits and thinks. Other times I just sits!"

There is much in contemporary society that encourages people to "just sit." For instance, television, the great burner up of time, disrupter of families, destroyer of conversation and substitute for intelligent thought. Or spectator sport, that exciting alternative to active participation. That escape mechanism from the cold world of reality to the fantasy world of the arena, where battles that are non-battles are fought before people evading the real battles they will never fight. The popularity of these contemporary thought substitutes is readily understandable, for thought can be painful, especially when there is little hope in the topics being considered.

In all fairness, valid relaxation is necessary and can be found in these areas. But when these things take the place of intelligent grappling with issues or become substitutes for necessary positive action, they become invalid and even dangerous.

Paul would have had something to say about it. In fact, he did speak to the issue. "Whatsoever things are true . . . think on these things" (v.8).

The word *think* is important; the Greek word used here has the connotation of thinking through logically and carefully. In fact, the same word is translated elsewhere in the New Testament as *account, reckon, reason, conclude.* Paul is not saying to *give casual thought,* but to *think seriously* about these things.

It ought to be obvious to any Christian that truth has been revealed by God to mankind in the person of Jesus Christ and through the medium of the inspired Word. This truth, which is eternal in character and vital in content, is not to be taken lightly, but to be assimilated thoroughly. This does not happen overnight. It takes a lifetime of careful, disciplined meditation and contemplation to even begin to grasp the immensity of the truth that God has for us. Therefore, a thoughtless Christian, devoid of meditation and contemplation, is a strange contradiction. He believes that he is heir to eternal truth which paradoxically he doesn't consider worth thinking about too seriously.

Focus Your Attention Carefully
"Whatsoever things are true" are to be matters of thought and contemplation. The Bible uses the idea of *true* in the sense of real.

Real as Opposed to Phony
And how important it is that we take note of this object of our thought life. There is so much confusion in many areas of our world that people are totally bewildered when they try to get at the truth of a matter. Some have become so disgusted and disillusioned that they have given up believing that there is any such thing as "reality" or any such people as "real people."

The young people have coined the term *plastic* to describe the people and society of the older generation. The disillusionment with politics and politicians has caused great concern in government because so many people feel that all politicians are phony and there is no point voting for any of them.

The Christian has another view. He believes in that which is real, and cannot afford to divert his attention to that which is phony. But he has to be careful, for the prevailing atmosphere of cynicism and despair can get to him.

Barnabas and Ananias are striking examples of men on different sides of this fence. Barnabas, a gracious man, was deeply influenced by his meditation on the things of God. He determined to sell his property and donate the proceeds to the church in Jerusalem. As far as we know, the only pressure to which he was subjected was the pressure of the Holy Spirit, and he responded positively to His promptings.

Ananias, on the other hand, was completely obsessed with thoughts of grandeur and captivated by visions of personal glory. These things upon which he focused his attention led him not to reality, but to disastrous phoniness.

The difference in destiny of these men is common knowledge. Barnabas went on to be a great man of the Word and encourager of the saints. Ananias died an ignominous death. But what we tend to overlook is the fact that their destinies were the product of actions and the actions were born of desires. Phoniness was the child of an attention focused on the phony, while reality was the offspring of a mind set on that which was real.

Paul goes on to add "things that are honest" to his list of valid thought objects. *Honest* is not the best translation of the word. Perhaps *noble and serious* would better convey the meaning intended.

Serious as Opposed to Frivolous

The Christian has no problems thinking seriously once he gets around to seriously thinking. Once he starts to think about the Lord his thought patterns inevitably lead to serious considerations. The grace of God is an overwhelmingly serious subject. If it were not for grace I would neither exist nor survive. Apart from grace I am lost and alone. Grace alone opens the arms of God and the gates of heaven. Grace leads me to repentance and faith, to commitment and service.

The call of God is a crushing thing. Called out of darkness into light; from death to life; from disaster to delight. Called to be a saint, an ambassador, a child of God and a joint heir with Christ. This is a serious business. The commission of God is vast as the ocean. The whole world to be reached. The church of God to be edified. The Word of God to be propagated. The purposes of God to be fulfilled. We could go on looking at the fundamentals of the faith and realize that there is not one basic of belief and thought that is not serious in the extreme.

Perhaps it is the very seriousness of our faith that frightens us into frivolous excess, simply because we feel that we can't cope with the solemnity of it all. Beware at this point, for only the serious-minded will do the will of God. The frivolous will do nothing more than pass the hours until they have no more to pass.

I do not speak against humor and laughter. They are divine inventions created for the well-being of human society. But their abuse, along with the fixation on trivia, has led many a Christian into the paths of impotence.

Moses and Aaron illustrate the point. Moses in the mountain, alone with God, was being made the recipient of God's law for His people. Meanwhile down in the valley Aaron and his people were having a party. Aaron fiddled while the mountain burned, and the people fiddled with him and finished up badly burned themselves.

To fill your mind with the frivolous at the expense of the serious is a mistake for any Christian to make.

Then Paul insists on his people thinking on "whatsoever things are just . . . " We are familiar with the biblical use of the words *justice* and *righteousness*.

Right as Opposed to Convenient
Humans have a deep-rooted need to be comfortable. From our earliest days our needs have centered around food in our stomachs, clothes on our backs, and a roof over our heads. Added to these physical necessities, we have well-developed emotional needs. Provided we are loved and appreciated, we will be more or less all right. All this is fine, but if we never grow past the idea that life is merely getting our own physical, psychological, and emo-

tional needs met, we will never develop into mature people. This lack of maturity is seen all too often in the lives of people who, when confronted with a choice, automatically choose that which is likely to give them the most comfort, whether it be in terms of material ease, social prestige or convenience. They have problems because their thought patterns have run on the track of what is most comfortable and convenient, rather than what is the right thing to do.

This is a desperate problem today. All too often decisions are made, not on the basis of what is admirable and noble, but on what is most expedient and profitable. It takes exercise of mind and devotion of life to get into the habit of wanting what is right. And if this devotion and exercise are not in evidence, there is a real chance that decisions will be made as a reflex action, not on the basis of convinced rightness, but on the basis of selfish convenience.

Joseph of Arimathea was a "just man," which means among other things that he wanted to do the right thing. In the city where he lived was another man who was something else: Pontius Pilate. Pilate was confronted with a decision that he wanted to evade and avoid. He tried every trick in the political book, the ecclesiastical book and the "P.R." man's book, but he still finished up with the silent Prisoner before him. He knew what was right, and he knew what would happen if he did it. He knew what was convenient and everything inside him screamed to do it. So he "washed his hands" of the matter and went to his grave responsible for his deed.

On the other hand, Joseph lived the rest of his days glad that he did what was right, not what was convenient. Begging for the body of the despised Jesus was not easy; taking this body in his own arms was no small thing; burying Him in his own tomb made Joseph a marked man. But it was the right thing to do and he did it!

Then there is "whatsoever things are pure."

Clean as Opposed to Dirty

I am sure that pornography quickly comes to mind, but while it is one aspect of that which is "not clean," there are other things that fit the bill, too. This needs to be said because many a saint who is anti-smut may be into some uncleanness himself.

David and Uriah are good examples of the two conflicting thought patterns. David sent his men to war and went to bed himself. That was a dirty trick. He saw his neighbor's wife and went to bed with her while the husband was in the service. That was a filthy trick. He got the woman pregnant and called the husband home on some pretext or other, assuming that the husband would spend the night at home and get David off the hook. That was a rotten trick.

When Uriah wouldn't go home, David got him drunk and that was a shabby trick; and when all else failed, he sent the man back to war with instructions that he should be liquidated. And that was unbelievable. All this was the product of a dirty scheming mind, but pornography was only a part of it and not even the beginning of it.

Uriah, on the other hand, was as clean as a whistle. He couldn't go home to his wife even for one night when his men were on the battlefield. Even when David, his king, got him drunk he had more moral stability than David had when he was sober.

Loving as Opposed to Discordant

This is what Paul is talking about in "whatsoever things are lovely . . . " Literally it means concentrate on things that promote brotherly love. Friction is not difficult to produce. Nobody has to take a course in learning how to do it. There is something about human nature that is adept at producing hostility and discord, and I think that thing is selfishness.

Many things happen to bring misunderstanding and conflict, but often things happen because they are made to happen by people who want them to happen. These people are set on discord and thrive on strife. You meet them in every walk of life. They are miserable people, and they make other people miserable, too. They have little idea of how to deal with issues, or how to handle sticky problems. They would rather fight than anything else, and they never have to look long to find a potentially explosive issue.

The Christian has no place in this kind of company. He is called to be a "peacemaker" and his special delight is to build bridges, not barriers; to throw bouquets, not bombs. Demetrius, the coppersmith of Ephesus, was set on disrupting his city, but the town clerk whose name we don't know (so we'll call him Anonymous) stilled the mob. The one was intent on wreckage and conflict, the other on peace and concord. What are you, a Demetrius or an Anonymous?

"Things that are of good report . . . " come next on Paul's food for thought menu.

Helpful as Opposed to Critical

To be destructively critical is to be caught in a web of chronic negativism. Unfortunately, many Christians find it their special joy and gift to be negative and critical about most things in general and many things in particular. They are like Tobiah and Sanballat who, when Nehemiah and Ezra were trying to rebuild Jerusalem, found fault with everything that was done.

Look for something helpful to say even if you can't agree with everything that is being done! If you have to disagree, do it in such a way that even your disagreement has helpful suggestions incorporated. Don't get so pessimistic that you see everything through black-tinted spectacles; and whatever you do, be careful how you sound when you speak.

When Jesus healed the demoniac in Gadara, the healed man went around ten towns giving a helpful message to all who would listen, and great blessing resulted. But did you notice the attitude of the Gadarenes? All they could think about was the fact that their pigs were now pork! Isn't it strange that some people can be so helpful and others so critical?

"If there be any virtue . . . " comes next. *Virtue* is not that which Victorian maidens defended. The word means *excellence*.

Excellent as Opposed to Inferior

It has been said somewhat sadly that if many Christians ran their businesses as they run their Christianity they would be broke in twelve months. This is because "nothing but the best" will do for the home and the business, but anything will do when it comes to service and worship. The great need for concentration on the excellent and rejection of the inferior is obvious.

"If there be any praise," think about that instead of what is wrong. It is not too difficult to speak long and often on, "What's wrong with our church?" Try something a little more difficult; give considerable thought to, "What's right with our church!" It may be difficult for you to do it because somebody you don't like may be doing something well. That's tough! Perhaps somebody you admire is making a disaster area out of the youth program. That's even tougher.

Positively as Opposed to Negatively

If you have trouble, remember Caleb and Joshua. They went with their friends to "spy out the land" and came back with their report. Caleb and Joshua had grapes and the rest had gripes. The two wanted to go ahead and do what needed doing, the rest wanted to forget the whole thing and ignore what they had been told to do. But Caleb and Joshua were right, and if you get into a positive frame of mind in terms of God's working in your life you will be right, too. But if you sink into the murky waters of pessimism you will sink without a trace.

Then we should listen to Paul's second major instruction. "Those things which ye have both learned, and received, and heard, and seen in me do" (v. 9). Space and time will not allow us to develop all the thoughts that are included in this remarkable verse, but Paul says . . .

Feed Your Minds Correctly

The perennial tension that exists between those who advocate feeding bodies and those whose concern is feeding minds is unfortunate. That people need food for their stomachs is obvious, and it goes without saying that those who have surpluses should give to those who do not have enough.

But people also need food for their minds, and the basis of all wholesome mind food is the truth of God. We have seen much of the truth that Paul taught, but in this verse Paul clearly outlines some of the methods he used.

Note the words, *learned, heard* and *seen.* To grow in spiritual and mental dimensions it is necessary to use the mind to learn, the ears to hear, and the eyes to see. Paul had given ample food for the minds of the Philippians through his intelligent presentation of the gospel in his teaching ministry; they had taken time to hear the Word of God preached; and (don't miss this) they had kept their eyes open to what he was doing as well as teaching and preaching.

Now those three methods are beyond reproach, and we do well to remember that to be correctly fed, a mind needs plenty of nourishment served through teaching, preaching and example. Make sure that you attend to the in-depth teaching of the Word. Don't be conspicuous by your absence when the Word is being exposited. Learn all you can from the example of those whom God has given you to be your leaders.

Finally, there is the little big word *do,* without which all that has gone before would be less than relevant. Thought, in its embryo form, is the result of that to which you give your attention; this comes to maturity through proper feeding. But it all comes to birth through action. Therefore, the smallest word *do* has the greatest importance.

The Lord Jesus said, "If ye know these things, happy are ye if ye do them" (John 13:17), and therein lies the secret. Blessing is the result of acting according to scriptural injunction in the enabling power of the Holy Spirit. So often we wonder why we are unblessed and why the river runs dry. The answer is not hard to find. If you do what you know, and what you know is the result of meditation on the truth of God taught to you in various ways, you will be blessed and be a blessing. But if you don't meditate and learn, you won't know what to do, and, therefore, you won't do much or be blessed. And even if you do know but don't do it, you will be unblessed. You will be a dismal archive of truth instead of a gallery of living experience.

Questions for Discussion

1. What comes to mind when you think on truth, honesty, justice, purity, loveliness, goodness, virtue, and praiseworthiness?

2. How has the church become plastic? What steps can be taken to make sure our faith is real?

3. What are you doing today to fulfill the commission of God?

4. How does the Christian's role as peacemaker affect his role at home, at work, in the community and in the world?

5. Do you balance your criticism with helpful suggestions for change? Are you as committed to helping people improve as you are to pointing out their shortcomings?

13

UNDER THE CIRCUMSTANCES

But I rejoiced in the Lord greatly, that now at the last your care of me hath flourished again; wherein ye were also careful, but ye lacked opportunity. Not that I speak in respect of want: for I have learned, in whatsoever state I am, therewith to be content. I know both how to be abased, and I know how to abound: every where and in all things I am instructed both to be full and to be hungry, both to abound and to suffer need. I can do all things through Christ which strengtheneth me.

Philippians 4:10-13

Have you ever asked someone, "How are you?" and received the response, "Well, under the circumstances . . . "? As the answer goes on it becomes increasingly obvious that the person really means it when he says he is "under the circumstances . . . "

Living Under the Circumstances
The Christian should never live under the circumstances, no matter how difficult the circumstances are.

Some people say, "You should live above your circumstances, not under them!" This worries me, because there is no way that you can live above them if they are part of your life. Maybe "living through them and triumphing over them" is what we should do.

As a boy during the Second World War, I was fascinated by the ships that sailed into the naval dockyard near my home. Some of them were so battered that they were almost completely waterlogged, while others were able to cut through the waves and storms with great momentum to fulfill their tasks. That's the picture I think we should keep in mind. Not sinking under or gliding over, but cutting through, keeping afloat and fulfilling our God-given tasks *in* the circumstances.

This appears to be what Paul was talking about in this passage. We are well aware of the circumstances of imprisonment that he was being subjected to, but here he raises another issue. He says, "But I rejoiced . . . greatly, that now at the last your care of me hath flourished again . . . " (v. 10).

The people in Philippi had become special friends of Paul, and when he had left their town they had taken it upon themselves to be partially responsible for his support. That meant financial and moral support. After some time the letters dried up and the support didn't come. For ten years this was the case. Imagine it! Total neglect for ten years, and no way of knowing why! There is no need to elaborate on the pain and disappointment that must have been Paul's experience, and there is little necessity to point out how desperately lonely he must have been.

As I have ministered to missionaries around the world, I have occasionally met those who left home with great resounding promises of support from their home churches. But the support dried up. They were left out on a limb. I have talked with heartbroken missionaries whose churches have cut them off because of some doctrinal nicety, or have just plain lost interest in them. They were very hurt, bewildered people. They were like men in battle who found themselves in the forefront of the fight, but way ahead of their supplies. These are circumstances of loneliness and hurt that come to only a few of us, but all of us have known disappointment and have had to cope. How well did we do?

Bitterness

Numerous reactions are available to hurt, lonely people. *Bitterness,* for example. I love the picture of family life that we have in Luke 10:38-42. It is a great encouragement to me to note that this was a household where the Lord felt at home and loved to visit. But it was very normal. The two sisters were so characteristic. Mary the mystic and Martha the caustic! The more mystical Mary became, the more caustic Martha became. She was a doer, and Mary was a dreamer. Praise the Lord for both, but be ready for trouble when they get near each other.

Mary wasn't lonely. She had Jesus to herself and "heard his word." But Martha was lonely, and she was bitter about it. Now presumably she could have taken a little time out of the kitchen and "sat at Jesus' feet," but she didn't. Maybe she had an "indispensability complex." "If I don't do it nothing will ever get done." And maybe she was right!

It is quite possible that if Martha had sat down for a

few minutes, she would not have been able to relax for thinking about all that wasn't getting done! She was one of those people who get ulcers while they relax! This is understandable, but her bitterness that stemmed from her self-imposed loneliness was inexcusable.

Heaviness

Another possible response to lonely circumstances is *heaviness*. In Psalm 102 there is an excruciating tale of woe. The Psalmist is almost overwhelmed with his circumstances and describes himself as "a sparrow alone upon the house top" (v. 7). What a picture of lonely heaviness and misery. There are few things that look as vulnerable and lonely as bedraggled sparrows sitting on the eaves of houses, with their tiny bodies apparently incapable of standing up to the ravages of the bitter weather. That's how the Psalmist felt. Alone, unloved, inadequate and miserable. So miserable that he couldn't even move into more amenable circumstances.

This kind of depression and heaviness is a frightening thing, as those who have experienced it will readily testify. Personally, I have known it only rarely, and for that I am thankful. I'm glad I've known it or I would have no idea of how depressed people were really feeling, but I'm glad I've known it rarely, for depression of that kind is something I can live without.

Selfishness

I think perhaps Elijah knew something of selfishness. Far be it from me to knock Elijah after he had taken on the priests of Baal and beaten them. The odds, incidentally, were 450 to 1. Then he had a threat on his life, and after that took off on a marathon run in the blazing heat. He ran from Carmel to Jezreel, then to Beersheba, then into the wilderness for another day. Well over 120 miles! I have done the same journey in an air-conditioned bus and felt tired, but he ran with a madwoman after him!

Far be it from me to criticize Elijah, but in his depression and loneliness he did get a bit too self-centered when he said, "And I, even I only, am left; and they seek my life, to take it away" (1 Kings 19:10). God had at least 7,000 of His people who had not succumbed to Baal.

How do you react to the lonely, hurtful, depressing times? With bitterness or heaviness or selfishness?

Paul had a different way of doing it. Immediately after he mentions the safe arrival of support from the people who had neglected him so long, he hastened to add that he understood that they had been unable to help, and that he had learned "in whatsoever state I am, therewith to be content" (v. 11).

There is an alternative to living "under the circumstances." It is living in them and cutting through them. There is an alternative to bitter, resentful reaction to distressing circumstances. It is learning in whatever state you are, to be content!

Content in My Circumstances

It must be stressed that contentment doesn't just happen. It has to be learned. Some people are more contented than others. They are as easy as old shoes; temperamentally they roll with the punches and come up calm and smiling. They are either born stoics or so phlegmatic that they take all that comes their way without grumbling or showing any sign of discomfort. But stay around long enough and something will get to them. Even they have to learn contentment sometimes.

Paul, however, was no stoic, and his temperament was hardly everybody's idea of the phlegmatic. So he really had to learn how to be content.

Aware of the Presence of God

Paul says in verse 9 that if Christians act according to

the principles he has enunciated in his teaching and shown in his living, "The God of peace shall be with you." This is a beautiful statement.

Peace has been defined as "the product of adequacy." This is a much more satisfying definition of peace than the more popular "absence of hostilities." We have all seen people who were under fire but completely at peace, whereas others have apparently been living in unclouded serenity but are breaking up inside. Hostilities or absence of hostilities are not the determinative factors in a person's peace of mind and heart. It is the presence or absence of resources that determines the peace or lack of it.

Paul talks, therefore, about the God of peace or the God of adequate resources. A few references to the "God of peace" will suffice to give us an overview of what Paul was talking about.

"And the God of peace shall bruise Satan under your feet shortly" (Rom. 16:20). This obviously refers to the great prophetic statement of Genesis 3:15 where God promised that the "seed" of the woman would bruise Satan's head and Satan would "bruise his heel." This was fulfilled in the triumph of Jesus our Lord over the forces of sin and hell, through His death and resurrection. But note that God has resources enough not only to do that but to bruise Satan under our heels, too. In other words, the resources of the God of peace are such that He, having bruised Satan through Christ's victory, can go on doing it through people alive in the world today.

Think of that next time you feel the temptation to bitterness because your circumstances are unfortunate. See the circumstances as being *permitted* by God, but *projected* by Satan. Then remember that the God of peace and adequate resources, who has already bruised Satan once through Christ, is about to do it again under your feet. Then try to be bitter or selfish! You might even get around to being content.

Or look, for instance, at this: "And the very God of peace sanctify you wholly; and I pray God your whole spirit and soul and body be preserved blameless unto the coming of our Lord Jesus Christ" (1 Thess. 5:23). This verse is thrilling, for it speaks of the overall competence of the God of adequate resources. So great is He that He has every intention of working on you, sanctifying and blessing you, until He has done all He wants to do with you down here. Then He plans to take you to be with Him at the coming of our Lord Jesus. In the interim He is able to "preserve" you. And that is worth knowing. Sometimes you can get so dejected that you think the roof is going to drop in and the floor is going to drop out. But listen to this. Even if they do drop in and out, He is able to "preserve" you until He is through with you down here, and He feels that you are ready for your promotion. That means so much to the troubled soul.

You may wish to look up some of the other references to the "God of peace" and apply them to your own education in the matter of being content.

Alert to the Purposes of God

There is a fascinating passage of Scripture in Lamentations 3. "It is good that a man should both hope and quietly wait for the salvation of the Lord. It is good for a man that he bear the yoke in his youth. He sitteth alone and keepeth silence, because he hath borne it upon him" (vv. 26-28). In this Scripture we read that God wants some people to get alone with their problems and stew in their juices for the simple reason that "He hath borne it upon him."

Make no mistake about this, for it is important. God wants you to be alone sometimes. He wants Paul to be neglected once in a while. If the Philippians come up with his monthly check year after year, Paul might forget whom he serves. If they keep looking after his every whim and caprice, Paul may grow blasé and flabby. So God allows a little neglect once in a while to remind him that it is God who is the source of his adequacy.

In our busy, pragmatic society quietness and aloneness are almost nonexistent. One of the scarcest commodities in the world today is quiet stillness. "Be still and know that I am God" (Ps. 46:10), certainly challenges us. But it is so contrary to our life-style that we don't even understand it or see the necessity for it. So God has to intervene sometimes and lay some aloneness or neglect or uncertainty on us so that we can get things into proper perspective again.

Imagine Paul in all his hurt remembering this, and fighting his feelings, and coming through to faith in the God of peace. Reckoning that God not only knew what He was doing, but also was in control of the situation.

Just suppose that your boat sank in the middle of the lake one day and nobody saw you. You couldn't swim, the water was cold and you were hanging on to the sodden rigging with fingers which were getting progressively colder and weaker. You would hardly be very contented.

On the other hand, suppose that as your boat was sinking, you radioed to shore. The rescue service picked up the message, told you to hold on and dispatched a helicopter immediately. You could see it in the distance, rapidly getting nearer. Would you feel more content? Of course you would, for you would see an end to your ordeal and you would feel confidence in your rescuers. That's how it is with the "God of peace." Instead of hanging on with growing despair and weakening fingers, you see the adequate resources and the infinite wisdom of your God at work, and you learn to be content because of what He is doing and the way He's doing it.

At the risk of being repetitious, I must remind you of the conditions under which it is possible to know that the "God of peace is with you." There are always conditions attached to the promises of God, and this promise is no exception. The conditions are basically that you should "do what you know," as we have already seen.

It is of vital importance that we should be alert to the basis upon which God is committed to act, particularly in the present age in which so many people want experiences of God but are not always prepared to get the experiences in the way that God demands. The existential influences of secular society have made inroads into Christian thinking and produced a generation of Christians who are so concerned about vital spiritual experience that they have little time for, or interest in, the doctrinal aspects of the Word.

It is understandable that we should have this trend at the present time, first, because it is a secular trend and the church loves to ape the world; and second, because Christians have traditionally been committed to doctrine and dogma that often did not get translated into shoe leather. The reaction against a Christianity that is doctrinaire but not alive is welcome, even if the impact of secular thinking is less than welcome. But, as with all reactions, we must be alert to possible overreaction. By all means pull the plug on the bath water, but make sure the baby doesn't go down the drain, too.

That is exactly what has happened in some areas. Because many Christians have for years been strong on basic doctrine and weak on love, the bath water of lukewarmness has been thrown out and along with it has gone the baby of doctrine. Away has gone the bath water of disgruntled, unattractive Christian living, but with it has gone the baby of biblical principle. This is a disaster of major proportions.

The power of the "God of adequate resources" is released in lives when people learn the biblical principles, obey them, mix them with faith, and see God work. As Paul puts it, "Those things which ye have both learned, and received, and heard, and seen in me, do: and the God of peace shall be with you" (v. 9). Faith in, and obedience to, the revealed will of God releases God's power in lives. Those who will go about it this way will experience the presence of God in superlative measure.

Confident in My Circumstances

There is another great truth in this passage concerning living with circumstances. Paul makes the remarkable statement, "I can do all things through Christ which strengtheneth me" (v. 13). The tone of this ringing truth is different from the tone in which he says, "I have learned . . . to be content." Contentment may be passivity that resembles a cow chewing her cud because she doesn't know what else to do. But this is no cud-chewing cow that speaks. It is the firebrand Apostle speaking with resounding confidence.

Some people have mistakenly interpreted this verse so that they really think they can do *anything*. They have claimed the promise and, accordingly, have assumed an air of omnipotence. A golden rule of Scripture is, "Read texts in their contexts." If you don't, you will come up with all kinds of theories and substantiate all manner of weird philosophies. Perhaps the oldest illustration of how unbiblical theories can be "proved" from the Bible is the theory that all Christians should kill themselves. If this sounds horrible, you're right. It is. It is totally anti-biblical. But listen to this. "Judas went out and hanged himself" (Matt. 27:5); "Go, and do thou likewise" (Luke 10:37); and "That thou doest, do quickly" (John 13:27). This is a patently ludicrous and extreme example, but it may serve to show that it is possible to "prove" that which is clearly unbiblical from the Bible. There is a safeguard against this. Take texts in their contexts and compare Scripture relating to a subject with others relating to the same subject.

To suggest a sense of omnipotence from Philippians 4:13, and to take this verse as a mandate for all kinds of behavior that clearly is not in line with God's purposes, is totally unsatisfactory. For example, I have met men without any preaching ability who claimed that through Christ they could preach because through Him they could do all things. This just isn't true, for it denies the Scriptures that state clearly that some are gifted and called in this area and others are neither gifted nor called. Uncalled and ungifted men must never expect to do "through Christ" that which Christ didn't call them or gift them to do! They may as well decide that "through Christ" they are going to make a million dollars if they think they can do all things through Him. But He may have no intention of letting them make a million because He knows it would be the worst possible thing for them.

Paul is not talking in broad unlimited generalities here. He is stating that whatever the circumstances God leads him into, he is confident that through the enabling of Christ he can do everything that needs to be done *in those circumstances.* And that is a great thing to believe!

Look at the circumstances he outlined . . . "I know both how to be abased, and I know how to abound: every where and in all things I am instructed both to be full and to be hungry, both to abound and to suffer need." He talks about the extremes of experience that he has known through the sovereign will of God, and he insists that in all these things he has been able to do "all things through Christ."

What would some of the "all things" be when he was "abased"? How do people cope with humbling circumstances? It is relatively simple to get very defensive when you are humbled, particularly if it happens in public! It is not difficult to blame someone else for your misfortune, or to try to shift to others the gaze of those witnessing your humiliation. Innuendo will do it. Plain old pride will insist on it and ego will work hard at it.

But Paul says, "I have learned to be totally confident that I can cope with it through Christ." He had learned the

secret of humility which is to see yourself as God sees
you. He had seen the example of humility in the Lord, who
had everything and held on to nothing, and he knew the
value of humility because he had discovered it to be the
doorway to reality. Therefore, he drew from the Spirit of
God the resources to cope with humbling circumstances.
He knew in his own heart the peace of not having to
defend or prove a thing. He simply let God work to His
own glory in the humiliation of His servant, as He had
done in the humiliation of His Son.

Of course, some people are humble and have no problem being humbled. They live in the shadows and prefer
them to the spotlight. Leave them alone, never ask them
to do anything, ignore them, or even exploit them, just as
long as you don't put them in a position of authority. They
couldn't cope with that. Paul could "through Christ." He
could be "abased" or he could "abound." Everyone's temperament will make it easier for him to cope with one or
the other, but not both. Coping with both does not come
naturally. It has to be learned!

I spoke in a missionary conference in which a young
surgeon bound for service in Africa was participating. I
was deeply impressed by this young man, for he knew
how to be abased and how to abound. For a number of
years he had worked in a top hospital, been a member of
the top clubs, made top money, and lived among the upper
crust of society. But God had called him to leave it all and
go to the needy people on the African continent.

The thing that really impressed me was that this doctor was asking people to support him financially. Have you
any idea what kind of a humiliating experience that can be?
To know that you can earn more than 99 percent of the
people listening to you through the skill and ability and
training in your own hands, and yet to be prepared to ask
those people to consider supporting you, and knowing that
most of them won't?

This young man could live in the rare atmosphere of upper crust society, enjoying the considerable financial rewards of his own work, and he could move quite happily in the wilds of Africa, depending, humanly speaking, on the sometimes fickle support of those at home who sent him.

Can you confidently approach both extremes and live in the limelight or the gaslight? Through Christ can you cope with being somebody or being nobody, whichever way it works out? That is the kind of thing that Paul is speaking about here.

The world is divided to some degree into the "haves" and the "have-nots." Some who start with nothing work hard and finish up with something. They tend to keep it that way. Others who have something sometimes have a crash on Wall Street and end up with nothing. They usually try to restore their previous situation. But Paul said quite confidently that he could move from one position to the other, whichever way it works out—"through Christ," of course. It was not a matter of great concern to him if he had things or didn't have them. Christ had taught him that. He held on to things so lightly that he could drop them as easily as he could drop his hat.

Some can do without things because they love the simple life. They have never known anything else. But give them a lot of something and they might go wild in an orgy of self-indulgence, or feel so guilty that they pretend that they don't have it. Others have so much of everything all their lives that they have the hardest time doing without things. But to have or have not, and to cope with both, is worth learning!

Some years ago I was eating in a restaurant in Denmark. It belonged to some delightful Christians who had invited me to take some meetings on the premises. Sitting just across from me were two American women who were on their first trip to Europe. They were unhappy about

their meal and were making things difficult for the waitress. I happened to know the waitress, and I also knew
the place that the ladies had come from in the U.S.A., and
I had great sympathy for both parties.

The women from America were used to such affluence
that they were incapable of adjusting to a new situation.
The waitress, on the other hand, had been born under the
Nazi occupation and had been reared in terrible circumstances where she had been grateful for anything she
could get her hands on. She was irritated by those who
needed abundance because she had never had it, while the
others were angry at something less than abundance
because they couldn't understand it. But what a difference
when you find someone perfectly at ease with either!

The Lord has every intention of giving us opportunities to grow, and I believe circumstances are one of His
favorite methods. If He can give us a big enough variety of
circumstances, and get us to accept them as from His gracious hand and as part of His educational program, He can
lead us on from strength to strength.

And talking of educational program, that is exactly
what it is, for Paul speaks of having *learned* and having
been *instructed*. The first word means *to be instructed* and
the second means *to be initiated into a secret*. It reminds
me of learning to swim. To be instructed involves all that
awful, but necessary, business of lying on the cold hard
tiles on the side of the pool learning how to move everything at the same time. But to be initiated is something
else! That means getting wet—and that's where the real
learning takes place.

Living in and through circumstances is not learned in
classrooms only, but where the action is. So learn your
lessons well from the Word, and then in the heat of the
battle be initiated into all that the Lord can be in your life
and all that you can accomplish as a result of His power and
presence.

I do not propose to deal with the way in which Christ is our strength, because we have seen on a number of occasions how the fact of the enabling power of the risen indwelling Lord in the person of the Holy Spirit constantly recurred in Paul's letter. All we need to say is that Christ alive within us can make us content and confident as we do what He tells us to do—and that is living!

Questions for Discussion

1. Are you living under, above, or through the circumstances of your life?

2. What has been your response to periods of loneliness? What do you find most helpful in overcoming loneliness?

3. When have you felt, like Elijah, that you were the only Christian left to make a stand? When you took your eyes off yourself, did you discover other faithful believers to support you?

4. What does it mean to be content in your circumstances? Are you content right now?

5. What opportunities for growth do you face right now? How do you think God will use them to help you mature?

14
SHARING

Notwithstanding, ye have well done, that ye did communicate with my affliction. Now ye Philippians know also, that in the beginning of the gospel, when I departed from Macedonia, no church communicated with me as concerning giving and receiving, but ye only. For even in Thessalonica ye sent once and again unto my necessity. Not because I desire a gift; but I desire fruit that may abound to your account. But I have all, and abound: I am full, having received of Epaphroditus the things which were sent from you, an odour a sweet smell, a sacrifice acceptable, well-pleasing to God. But my God shall supply all your need according to his riches in glory by Christ Jesus. Now unto God and our Father be glory for ever and ever. Amen. Salute every saint in Christ Jesus. The brethren which are with me greet you. All the saints salute you, chiefly they that are of Caesar's household. The grace of our Lord Jesus Christ be with you all. Amen.

Philippians 4:14-23

Being practical and spiritual at the same time is like trying to pat your head with your right hand while rubbing your tummy with your left. If you aren't very careful you find both hands doing the same thing. Some people are all spiritual and others are all practical. The former are "so heavenly minded they are no earthly use . . . " and the latter are "so earthly minded they are no heavenly use . . . " Somehow Christians have got to get both things operating.

In the last chapter we saw how Paul had a tremendous spiritual concept, namely: "I can do all things through Christ which strengtheneth me" (Phil. 4:13). But immediately he says, "Notwithstanding ye have well done, that ye did communicate with my affliction" (v. 14). He is saying that while it is true spiritually that Christ equips him for life and ministry, there is also a practical side to this equipping. And that is done by people like the Philippians. There is no doubt in Paul's mind that Christ equips spiritually as people minister practically, and He achieves His divine ends through human means. In this particular instance the divine end is the providing for Paul's needs and the human means are the people who share.

This is something that we do well to remember. I wonder sometimes if we realize how important our cooperation on a practical level is to the outworking of God's plans on a spiritual level. Do we realize how much the flow of divine blessing is channeled by the degree of our sharing? Consider this subject of sharing as we study how the Philippians brought this blessing to Paul.

The Point of Sharing

Paul says, "Ye did communicate with my affliction" (v. 14). This is a telling statement. He had some needs that were so great that he called them "an affliction." He tells the Philippian believers that when he first left Philippi and went on to Thessalonica they were the only ones who shared with him. But then even their support ceased and so he had found himself without any visible means of support. He felt rather like a soldier who, having advanced way ahead of his supporting services, found his food running low and his ammunition depleted and no radio contact. A pretty unpleasant situation!

No doubt some pious saints back home might have said, "Great. It will give him a chance to trust the Lord. This will test his faith. Now we'll find out how his commitment can stand up to a real test." And they would have been right. But they might have forgotten that trusting the Lord to provide gives the Lord the opportunity to show His adequacy. And He does this through involved people.

It is sad, but true, that Christians have been known to tell the naked and the hungry to be warm and fed, but have done no warming and feeding. In fact, we have even tended to criticize the unfortunate for getting into such a state. Instead of being God's answer we have intensified man's problem.

The Philippians had shared at the point of Paul's need. There is a sharing that is not at the point of need. For example, the sharing of a convivial evening with friends on the understanding that they will return the compliment is one kind of sharing. It is good and valid, but sharing at the point of need often involves sharing where there is little or no possibility of return. Because of this there is no doubt about the motivation for the sharing. It is a loving, caring, sacrificial action.

But how can this kind of sharing happen? I would suggest three stages. First, there is the *identification* of need, then *interest* in the need, followed by *involvement* in meeting the need.

The story of the Good Samaritan comes to mind. (See Luke 10:30-37.) When the priest came to the place where the unfortunate man lay half dead he identified his need. It was plain to see. The man was "half dead" and left in that condition would soon be "whole dead."

The Levite did better than the priest, however, for he not only identified the need of the man but he also showed interest in his need. He "came and looked on him." While his reaction to the situation was far superior to the priest's reaction, it was still far from adequate.

Then came the Samaritan and, like his predecessors, he identified the need. Like the Levite, he showed interest in the need. But, unlike both of them, he became involved in the need. It takes all these ingredients to produce real sharing.

The Principles of Sharing

I am a firm believer in the enunciation of "principles" in Christian experience. Sometimes it gets a little onerous and people can get a little impatient. They don't want to go into principles; they want to get on with the practical. They aren't interested in knowing how a thing works, just so long as it works. That is fine as far as it goes, but it doesn't go far enough. When your car will start and run, who cares about how or why it runs! But when it won't start in the middle of the night, in the middle of nowhere, in the middle of a snowstorm, you'll find yourself in the middle of a mess if you don't know how it works.

That's how it is with Christian experience. While it goes, it's fine; but when it doesn't, you should know why it doesn't. And the only way to know is to be thoroughly acquainted with the principles.

We are talking about sharing, but perhaps you only share when you feel like it, are pushed into it, or are incapable of getting out of it.

That kind of sharing is desperately limited, and nothing is going to change until you are motivated to share from a sound understanding of the why and the how of it all.

Paul gives a clue to the principle of sharing in the expression, "giving and receiving" (v. 15). Do you remember the words of our Lord, "freely ye have received, freely give" (Matt. 10:8)? Immediately we see that sharing is not related to personal inclination or applied pressure, but to the grace of God. If God has given to you freely, you are expected to give equally freely. The principle strikes at the very root of selfishness, for it insists that if you expect God to go on being gracious to you, then you must do what He expects you to do. And He expects you to give! Sharing is a response of loving obedience motivated by the good news of God.

Then, there is the further teaching of our Lord, "Give, and it shall be given unto you" (Luke 6:38). Now we are all aware that giving is governed by receiving. If we don't have it we can hardly be expected to give it. But the Lord also said that the converse is true. Receiving is governed by giving. If we give, we'll get. This tends to strain our belief, but it is a scriptural and spiritual fact.

Some churches and individual Christians make an annual faith promise to the Lord to give a certain amount to world missions. They do not promise to give what they know they can afford. They are not calculating their "tithe after taxes." They are believing God to show them a figure that they anticipate by faith He will enable them to give. They are giving what they don't have, believing that they will have it because God says, "Give and it shall be given." Give it and you'll receive it! I have no doubt that this approach will sound almost unbelievable to some of you, but I can assure you it is part of the divine principle of sharing.

I was asked to speak at a World Missions Conference in Park Street Church, Boston, Massachusetts. The people in that church that week covenanted with God to give $400,000 to world missions, believing that God would enable them to do it. And He will.

Let me hasten to add that this principle does not operate solely in financial matters. It works in all other areas of sharing.

But there is something else that we must remember about sharing. "Give, and it shall be given unto you; good measure, pressed down, and shaken together, and running over" (Luke 6:38). This is a lovely verse. If we get around to sharing, we get back far more than we give. The non-sharer finds this hard to believe, but it's true. We may give somebody a figurative bushel of grain, but in return we will get a bushel heaped up, shaken down, spilling over. Grain all over the place! This is all part of the principle of sharing.

Years ago I joined a book club so that I could get a copy of a new four-version Bible. There was some delay in the processing of my membership application; when it was finally completed, it was too late for me to get the book I wanted. I wrote to the club, asking them to try hard to find me a copy of the book; and to my delight, they succeeded. The day after my new Bible arrived so did a friend of mine. He was heading out to Borneo to do Bible translation work. Something inside me said, "Give Ian your Bible. It will be invaluable to him in Borneo." Now, I knew that it would probably be more valuable to him than to me, but I had worked so hard for that Bible that I just didn't want to part with it. Finally, I told my friend, "This is my new Bible, it was the last one available, it is a unique edition, and I'm so thrilled with it. And I think God has told me to give it to you, and I don't want to!"

I expected him to be a gentleman, even if I wasn't! I hoped he would say, "Oh, really, Stuart, I couldn't take that, knowing how much it means to you."

But he didn't. He said, "Thanks, that will be a marvelous help in my translation work. I was hoping you would give it to me!" And off he went to Borneo with my Bible under his arm!

The next day an identical Bible appeared on my desk. A colleague saw me looking at it and said, "It's yours."

"No," I replied, "mine is on the way to Borneo."

"I don't know what you're talking about," he answered, "but I got two copies in the mail yesterday, and the Lord told me to give one to you!"

So I had my Bible, Ian had his Bible, Borneo got a translation tool, I had the joy of being obedient and the thrill of sharing (albeit reluctantly), and once again I received because I gave, and I got much more than I shared!

The Persistence of Sharing

"Once and again" (v. 16), they gave. Over and over they gave. It seems that whenever Paul needed to use an illustration of sharing he thought of the Philippians. When he wrote to the Corinthians to scold them for their poor record in this respect, he gave the Philippians glowing praise. They had been persistent and consistent, sacrificial, generous, reliable and thoroughly motivated in their sharing. They did it, not out of abundance, but out of poverty.

Peter and John were confronted by a lame man at the Beautiful Gate of the Temple. He was busy begging from the worshipers when he caught Peter's attention. "Silver and gold have I none; but such as I have give I thee," said Peter (Acts 3:6).

It would have been easy for Peter to nudge John as he heard the poor man beg and say, "Hey, have you got anything to give him? I'm broke."

And I can well imagine John replying, "So am I. I'll bet he could lend us a dime or two!" And so, with a chuckle, they could have passed off the awkward moment. But they didn't, because they had learned to persist in the sharing of what they had. And so the lame man was blessed more than he had dreamed. He asked for alms and got legs!

The Product of Sharing

Read what it says in verse 17: "Not because I desire a gift: but I desire fruit that may abound to your account." Now if this wasn't inspired Scripture I think I would be inclined to be a little cynical at this point. Can you imagine anyone saying, "Now, friends, we are going to give you an opportunity to share with us. Not so that we might benefit, but in order that you might benefit. It's not us we are thinking about. It's you!" I think that I would be as disinclined to believe that as I was disinclined to believe my Dad when, after tanning my hide, he said, "Son, this hurts me more than it hurts you."

But hold it a minute. Could it really be that the Spirit of God through the Apostle is trying to teach us something? Is there any reason to believe that the giver benefits from his giving? Yes, there is!

Did you know that records are kept of your Christian life? Are you aware that your sharing, for instance, is recorded like an account? For that is exactly the term that Paul uses. Note how he talks about "abounding to your account." And if that isn't enough you should always remember that your sharing will be rewarded in heaven. In Matthew 10:42 we are told that if we share something as commonplace as a cup of cold water we shall under no circumstances lose our reward. So the only way to lose when it comes to sharing is to fail to share. If you share it will be recorded and rewarded.

What a delightful thing it is to be able to say that you want to persuade people to share so that they might benefit! How much more willing people would be to share themselves if they realized that sharing is more than a duty, it is a pleasure.

The Pleasure of Sharing

We don't have any problems understanding the pleasure that Paul had in receiving what the Philippian Christians had sent to him by Epaphroditus. But when it comes to real sharing it's not the receivers alone who derive pleasure. Can you imagine what joy the Philippians experienced when they heard their sharing described as "an odour of a sweet smell, a sacrifice acceptable . . . " (v. 18)?

Now, it's possible that Epaphroditus had said to the congregation one Sunday morning, "Okay, folks. What about old Paul? The poor old codger is having it rough in Rome, so what about a little offering for him? Let me suggest your loose change." It is possible but highly improbable, for these people were really engaging in spiritual service when they did practical things. They had learned to "first (give) their own selves to the Lord" (2 Cor. 8:5). Once they had done that, all that they gave of themselves was unto Him no matter its earthly destination. What a joy to be able to give on that basis!

My mother-in-law is one of the most incorrigible givers that I have ever met. She just enjoys giving. It is her hobby and her passion. Sometimes it's a little difficult because she loves giving so much that when we try to give in return she isn't interested in that at all. She has even been known to ask us not to give her anything because she derives all her joy in giving. Now you have heard many men talk about their mothers-in-law, but have you ever heard that kind of testimonial before?

There was an awful lot of pleasure in Rome and Philippi over the whole sharing experience, but it was nothing to the joy in heaven. Don't miss what Paul says about sharing. It was "well-pleasing to God."

Have you ever wondered what pleases God? Nothing pleases Him more than to see His children getting more like His Son. He was so thrilled with His only begotten Son that He decided to make many more like Him and bring them to glory. It's a long, slow process, of course, but He's doing it nevertheless. When selfish people start sharing, it is an evidence of Christlikeness, because that was what He was . . . a sharer. Every time you share you sacrifice, and with loving sacrifice God is well pleased. It reminds Him of His Son and shows the impact His Spirit is having in making people more like His Son. Sharing brings great joy to receiver, giver and heavenly observer!

The Price of Sharing

As we have already seen, Paul uses the terms "acceptable sacrifice" to describe sharing, and we must not overlook this. It's a bittersweet sort of thing. The joy and the delight are sweet but the sacrifice can be bitter. "Giving till it hurts" is not an evangelical cliché. It is a missing ingredient in contemporary Christian society.

The joys of a fruitful ministry are sweet, but the means of attaining it are bitter. As I have traveled the world and seen God work it has been sweet, but many a lonely hour away from home and family has been the price. And it has been bitter at times. The young people in our church recently produced a musical worship experience, and they enjoyed doing it. But one day their rehearsal coincided with the National Basketball Association championship game between Milwaukee and Boston. Leaving the TV to go to the rehearsal was tough, and I will not easily forget my 15-year-old son having his first lesson in the price of sharing. He went backward out of the room, clutching his guitar and watching till the very last second. But he made it!

The Prospects of Sharing

The best-known verse in this section is verse 19: "But my God shall supply all your need according to his riches in glory by Christ Jesus." What does this mean? It means that God is committed to seeing that the sharer doesn't suffer because he shares. This is good news, because so often at the back of our minds we think that we can't afford to share when the real truth of the matter is that we can't afford not to share. "God is no man's debtor" is a truism. I like it. "You can't outgive God" is another, and I like that one, too. Because it's biblical.

When I was a bank inspector I traveled first class, stayed in good hotels, ate well and ran up some fair-sized bills. But I did it with great peace of heart because the bank was behind me picking up the tab. I like sharing because whatever I share I know God is coming right behind picking up the tab. He's committed to meeting my needs.

On occasion the bank was known to question some expenditure, and some of my colleagues were not reimbursed for certain questionable claims. But there is no possibility of God failing to come through in any way.

The word *supply* means *fulfill,* and that is how God operates with sharing saints. He never does less than fulfill His Word; and for Him to fulfill is to fill full. He always does it His way, too, "according to his glorious riches." He does it in a way that brings glory to Himself.

To give "according to" is different from giving "out of." God doesn't give in any other way than "according to his glorious riches." The billionaire who gives twenty dollars to a famine relief fund is giving "out of" his wealth, but what difference does twenty dollars make to him? He doesn't even notice it! He has given out of, but no according to, his wealth. Always remember the way that God reimburses the sharing person. He will never be skimpy or shoddy, but will always act in a way that is compatible with His Being.

The prospects are therefore extremely bright for the person who shares. God is committed to looking after him, and doing it in a way that measures up to His standing and status. He does it through Christ Jesus.

Paul gets so excited about the contemplation of these truths that he bursts out, "Now unto God and our Father be glory for ever and ever. Amen." And in the light of all that we have seen in the Epistle to the Philippians, may I recommend a similar response from you, too?

Questions for Discussion

1. What are some ways of being practical and spiritual at the same time?

2. Does your response to needy people provide God's answer or intensify their problems?

3. What is your motivation for sharing your life and resources with others?

4. What resources—money, time, materials—can you give to help further the kingdom today?

CONTACTOUSLY

~~Contactac~~